In the

QUARANTINE KITCHEN

... how we all became chefs during a pandemic.

A collection of recipes, photos, and stories from the year 2020.

DANIELLA, KRISTINA, and TRACI CANGIANO

In the Quarantine Kitchen - A collection of recipes, photos, and stories from the year 2020.

Copyright © 2020 Daniella Cangiano, Kristina Cangiano, and Traci Cangiano

Second Printing 2021

Cover design, book design, and layout by Gina Laiso, Integrita Productions

Library of Congress Control Number: 2020919837

International Standard Book Number: 978-0-578-73722-5

Printed in the United States of America.

For the brave front line workers who carried us through the coronavirus pandemic.

We thank you for your courage and fearlessness in the face of the unknown.

DANIELLA, KRISTINA, and TRACI CANGIANO
Founders of the Quarantine Kitchen

Daniella is a full-time college senior. She has been a baker her entire life but learned so much more during this year's months of quarantine. Cooking and baking have become a couple of her favorite hobbies in the last few months. She also spends her time working an internship part-time and studying for her law school entrance exam. She loved helping to build the Quarantine Kitchen cookbook alongside her mom and sister.

Kristina is a high school senior. During the quarantine, she discovered her love for fashion and design, beginning with making masks for friends and family. While she did spend lots of time in the kitchen both cooking and taste testing, she spent a lot of time crafting and creating as well. She is looking forward to soon choosing a college for a design-related program! Kristina also loved helping her mom, Traci, and sister, Daniella, compile recipes to put in the Quarantine Kitchen cookbook. She is most excited to try them all out!

Traci is a wife, mom, and busy broker/owner of a local real estate company, Cangiano Estates, Ltd. This lifelong Staten Islander has philanthropy in her veins, from helping the community head on after Superstorm Sandy ravaged SI to working closely with individuals in need whenever necessary. Notably, Traci assisted in securing funding for a van for two handicapped children so the family did not have to bear the financial burden. When COVID-19 struck their community, Traci and her girls started the Quarantine Kitchen page, but they never expected it to grow the way it has. Once it did, they knew they had to turn a negative situation into a positive. Members from all over the world have said, time and time again, how much peace and happiness the page had brought to them. Traci and her girls are elated that they are able to give back and hand the proceeds from the sale of this book to the Siller Foundation/Tunnel to Towers Covid19 Heroes Fund, for the front line heroes.

For the amazing guidance through the self-publishing book process, meticulous layout design, and extreme patience throughout this journey, we would like to thank Gina Laiso of Integrita Productions.

Thank you to Kathi Toro for offering a fresh set of eyes to proofread this cookbook.

Thank you Vinny Cangiano, cutting board master, for your hours in the shop helping to make our friends in the Quarantine Kitchen smile.

The biggest thank you goes out to the 35k (and still growing) members of the Quarantine Kitchen. Without all of you, this book would have never happened. Thank you for being a part of the largest distraction we all needed during our time in quarantine. Who would have ever thought …

In loving memory of Zak, who quickly became our QK mascot. You became a bright light daily during a very dark time.

Thank you Daniella. ♥

From the Quarantine Kitchen of
Daniella Cangiano

I do not think any of us were prepared for what was coming: a pandemic. Our busy lives came to a screeching halt and we didn't really know what to do in a situation like this. My social media feeds were full of panic and hysteria. Anxiousness came over me every time I read an article or turned on the news. The uncertainty of what the future would hold haunted my family. Whether it was our Italian tendencies or our natural defense mechanisms, we started to buy a bunch of food, just in case. My mom bought 40 pounds of pasta!

In almost a magical way, we fell into a routine. We began a journey inside our own homes. Not just in my home, but all over the globe. Millions of closets were cleaned, artists and creators were inspired, passion projects finally got the attention they deserved, and I know for sure that we all had one thing in common: At the end of a long day, we all ended up in the kitchen.

As the four of us sat down for dinner one night during the first week of the New York City lockdown, my mom shared a passing thought, "Everyone must be doing the same thing as we are. Why don't we start a Facebook group where we can all share what we're cooking every day? We all have to eat, right?" And, so, Quarantine Kitchen was born. In just a few days, we reached a thousand kitchens. Then, it grew to 5,000. After a month, we reached 20,000 kitchens. Now, our group has more than 35,000 members. With members from every inch of the world, we truly went on a journey without leaving our homes.

Unintentionally, too, we created a giant family. Each day we'd cook together and eat together. Handwritten recipes that were passed down from relatives have been shared and made and… made again. We were all home with our families during a time of such uncertainty, but we created our own "quarantined" group. We shared everything from daily meals to holiday traditions.

On our journey, we met lots of remarkable individuals, many of whom were the very people protecting our health and safety. Members of the group applauded essential workers when they had the opportunity. We saw an outpouring of charity and support from meals sent to firehouses to cookie care packages for nursing home residents. I was honored to have been able to see all of this good unfolding, during such a trying time. If nothing else, Quarantine Kitchen caused a much-needed distraction to the chaotic outside world.

Looking back, 2020 was not what anyone expected it to be. I never thought I would be sitting at my computer during quarantine writing a preface to a cookbook! But I'm thankful that I have been a part of such a positive distraction, a sentiment that is shared by many members of our group. I hope that by the time you are reading this, the coronavirus pandemic is a distant memory. I hope that the time you spent at home during the months of lockdown was not just filled with uncertainty and panic, but, more importantly, love, family, and food.

Being confined to the kitchen wasn't so bad. Our very own Quarantine Kitchen baked hundreds of cookies for friends, cooked Sunday dinners, and chilled quite a few bottles of wine. At the end of the day, when we emerged from our home offices and makeshift classrooms, we sat down at the kitchen table and ate together. I think we all had more family dinners in the last few months than we ever had before! These are the pandemic memories I will always cherish.

From the Quarantine Kitchen of
Maria Martarella

For me, there is nothing more visual than a beautiful food presentation. I am no food critic; however, my love of cooking is no secret. I am a Sicilian girl from an old-fashioned family who embraces my family's recipes, which are treasured. Preparing those recipes allows me to go back to moments cooking with my grandmother or sharing an amazing feast with the ones I miss. Now, I have the opportunity to share my passion, for what I call magical food, with everyone. Set the table, have people gather in the kitchen, and pour a glass of wine. Get ready to share a memory with the ones you love.

TABLE OF CONTENTS

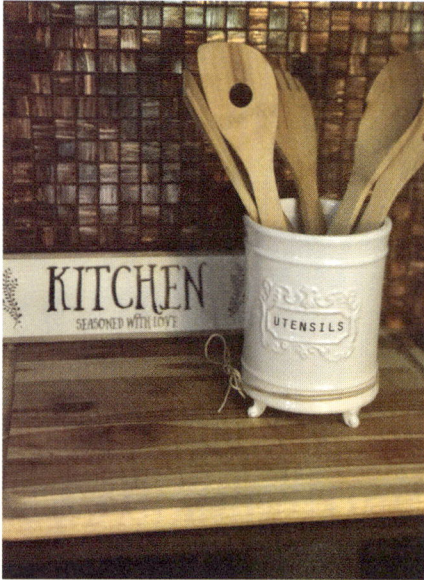

OUR QUARANTINE KITCHENS

BREAKFASTS

We were up at the crack of dawn.

From the Quarantine Kitchen of
Judy Sommerich

Unfortunately, I don't have a picture of the Strata and won't be making it since it easily feeds 10 (I'm single). If it weren't for the quarantine I'd happily make it for my sister and nieces or for my friend Andrea and her family since they were my guinea pigs for the recipe the first time I made it. However, due to the quarantine I'm unable to see my sister, nieces, or my friend Andrea and her family. (Have I mentioned how much I hate quarantine??!?!)

The background of the Strata is that I started making it 12+ years ago to bring to my friend Andrea's Christmas Tree Trimming Party. My mother was Italian and my father was Jewish. Andrea is Jewish and her husband is Italian so it just fit ... if you know what I mean. Andrea was convinced her daughter Rachel, who was 7 at the time and a very picky eater, wouldn't eat it and had planned to make her macaroni and cheese but, lo' and behold, when I walked into her apartment, carrying the Strata (still warm and aromatic), Rachel looked at it, sniffed it a good 2 to 3 times, looked at me inquisitively, and said, "there's sausage in there, right?" I nodded and she stood in the kitchen with her hands on her hips, trying to decide if she should taste it. After a few minutes she said, "May I have a piece with sausage?" So, I cut her a tiny piece. She took one bite and went running into the living room and shouted, "Mom, forget the macaroni and cheese, I'm eating Aunt Judy's sausage cake."

Love Quarantine Kitchen. Honestly, you have been a savior to me for the last several weeks. We've been hit hard and it's been daunting for all of us. Thank you for adding some lightness to the dark times.

Hugs from Da Bronx!

INGREDIENTS

1 tablespoon vegetable or olive oil, plus more for greasing the pan

1 – 1 ½ pounds Italian sausage, removed from casings and crumbled (or turkey sausage)

1 ½ cups onion, small dice (or 2 leeks cleaned and finely diced)

¾ cup red bell pepper, small dice

¾ cup yellow or orange bell pepper, small dice

8 ounces of baby bella or white button mushrooms, sliced thin

1 pound zucchini, sliced into ¼ inch thick slices and into half-moon shape

2 teaspoons salt

1 tablespoon chopped fresh marjoram leaves (or 1 teaspoon dried)

1 tablespoon chopped fresh oregano leaves (or 1 teaspoon dried)

1 tablespoon fresh chopped Italian parsley (or 1 teaspoon dried)

1 pound Italian bread or French bread, cut into ½ inch cubes (8 cups more or less)

12 ounces shredded mozzarella (or fontina cheese)

¾ cup Parmigiana (or Romano)

10 eggs (or the equivalent amount of egg substitute)

1 cup half-and-half

1 cup milk (either whole, 1%, or 2%)

1 cup low sodium chicken broth

½ teaspoon freshly ground black pepper

BREAKFAST STRATA WITH ITALIAN SAUSAGE, ZUCCHINI & BELL PEPPERS

Preheat the oven to 350°F. Lightly grease a 9x13 inch baking dish with cooking spray or oil.

Heat a 12 inch sauté pan over medium heat. Add the sausage and cook, stirring and breaking the meat into small pieces, until lightly browned, 8 to 9 minutes. Transfer to a paper towel lined plate to drain.

Add 1 tablespoon oil to the same pan & increase the heat to medium-high. Add the onion (or leek), red and yellow (or orange) bell pepper, sliced mushrooms, zucchini, and ¼ - ½ teaspoon of salt, and sauté until the vegetables are just tender, about 4 minutes. Add the herbs and stir to combine. Transfer to a plate to cool.

In a medium mixing bowl, combine the cooled sausage and vegetables and gently mix to combine.

Spread 4 cups of the bread cubes in the bottom of the prepared baking dish. Top with half of the sausage and vegetable mixture. Sprinkle with half of the mozzarella (or fontina) and half of the parmesan (or Romano). Repeat with the remaining bread, sausage/vegetable mixture and cheeses.

In a medium mixing bowl, whisk the eggs (or egg substitute), milk, half-and-half, stock, pepper, and remaining salt. Pour the egg mixture evenly over the top of the casserole. Make sure you cover as much of the bread as possible.

You can either cover the casserole with plastic wrap and store it in the fridge or bake it immediately for approximately 1 hour, until it has cooked through, the cheese has melted, and the top is golden and a nice crust has formed. Let the strata rest for 10-15 minutes before slicing and serving.

Some Tweaks to Consider:
- If you don't like zucchini, it's out of season, or is overpriced, substitute with fresh steamed broccoli or 2 boxes of thawed, frozen chopped spinach (drained well).
- If you don't like mozzarella (Who doesn't like mozzarella I ask you?) you can substitute with cheddar or Swiss. (I've made versions with both cheddar and Swiss and both were hits.) Tip: I add approximately 1 teaspoon of dried mustard to the custard when I use cheddar or Swiss to give a little kick.

From the Quarantine Kitchen of
Cindy Watson

I cook. As often as I can, in a variety of ways. Cooking centers me. After a long day, a stressful week, coming into the kitchen to create a meal that is nourishing and delicious feeds my soul and spirit.

Since COVID-19 changed our lives, I have had the privilege to cook almost every night. Working from home, mostly, and only going into the church on Tuesday afternoon and Sunday morning has changed my rhythm, but not my love of cooking.

My family loves my cooking and for my grand-children, I am "the cooking grandma." One of my grandsons wanted to cook with me. Specifically, he wanted to make granola. I have a great recipe I have adapted from several I have seen. Cooking with grandma is not easy when you live 800 miles apart.

What a gift technology is for this season. Google hangouts became our "friend" and for that first time, we set up a time and we made granola together!

We are now cooking together at least once a week. Often granola, and sometimes gluten-free cookies. My grandson doesn't "need" me to make granola, what he needs, what I need is time together. We talk, we laugh, he sometimes plays his violin, we share the weather and the plans for the day.

Cooking connects us, encourages us to be a community in whatever way we can.

INGREDIENTS

⅓ cup canola, vegetable or safflower oil

⅓ cup maple syrup or honey

½ teaspoon ground cinnamon

½ teaspoon salt

3 cups old-fashioned rolled oats

1 cup sliced almonds (or walnuts or pecans)

1 cup dried fruit (cranraisins, dried apricots or diced dates or figs, raisins or a combination of dried fruits)

HOMEMADE GRANOLA

Heat the oven to 300°F and line a rimmed sheet pan with parchment paper.

In a large bowl whisk or stir together oil and honey (or maple syrup), cinnamon and salt until thoroughly mixed.

Add the oats and almonds (or other nuts) and mix together. Stir to coat well. It is okay if it is clumpy.

Transfer to the sheet pan and spread out into an even layer, use a spatula or wooden spoon to press down if necessary.

Put in the oven and bake for 10 minutes and then stir the mixture. Bake for 10 more minutes and check. It will still feel "wet" coming out of the oven, just make sure the almonds are toasted. You will be able to smell them. You might need to bake for another 5 minutes.

Add the dried fruit by sprinkling across the granola ... press it in. Let cool. Once cool, break it apart and put in a Ziploc bag or container.

Enjoy!

From the Quarantine Kitchen of
Christine Kanarick

With no flour, no butter, and no oil, these banana oatmeal muffins with chocolate chips (or carob chips) are made in the blender and are moist, healthy, and delicious!

INGREDIENTS

2 cups oats, quick-cooking or old-fashioned

2 large, very ripe bananas

2 large eggs

1 cup plain nonfat Greek yogurt (you can use dairy-free yogurt or ¾ cup nondairy milk to make this a dairy-free recipe)

2 to 3 tablespoons honey (can be omitted for a less sweet muffin)

1 ½ teaspoons baking powder

½ teaspoon baking soda

1 teaspoon pure vanilla extract

⅛ teaspoon kosher salt

Up to ½ cup mix-ins: chocolate chips (mini or regular), chopped dark chocolate, Carob chips, nuts, dried cranberries, or blueberries (fresh or frozen and rinsed)

OATMEAL BANANA BLENDER MUFFINS

Preheat the oven to 400°F. Lightly grease a 12-cup standard muffin tin or line with paper liners. If using liners, lightly grease them as well. Set aside.

Place all ingredients but the mix-ins in a blender or the bowl of a food processor fitted with the steel blade: oats, bananas, eggs, Greek yogurt, honey, baking powder, baking soda, vanilla extract, and salt. Blend or process on high, stopping to scrape down and stir the ingredients once or twice as needed until the batter is smooth and the oats have broken down almost completely, about 3 minutes. By hand, stir in the mix-ins.

Divide the batter among the prepared muffin cups, filling each no more than three-quarters of the way to the top. Sprinkle with additional chocolate chips or nuts as desired. Bake for 15 minutes, until the tops of the muffins are set and a toothpick inserted in the center comes out clean. Place the pan on a wire rack and let the muffins cool in the pan for 10 minutes. They will deflate but still taste delicious.

Remove from the pan and enjoy!

• These can be frozen for up to 2 months.

From the Quarantine Kitchen of
Grace Maiorano

As Italians during the holiday seasons, there's always plenty of Panettone leftover. These are easy ways to kick it up a notch with your leftovers.

INGREDIENTS

I use original Panettone with candied fruit and raisins

Other Filling Suggestions:
Apricot preserves
Orange preserves
Sliced Banana

Coconut Rum Raisin
Add shredded coconut to cream cheese frosting and one teaspoon of coconut extract. Drizzle rum over Panettone layers and glaze the top and add coconut and raisins.
   Glaze: Combine 1 cup powdered sugar and 1 to 2 tablespoons of milk or water, enough to thin the glaze to desired consistency for drizzle.

Berry Shortcake
Cool Whip and fresh fruit. Spread a thin layer of raspberry or strawberry jelly between layers.

Nutella Amaretto
Drizzle Amaretto over Panettone layers filled with Nutella. Nuts optional.

Tiramisu Trifle
Soak layers of Panettone with coffee (espresso) and add vanilla pudding filling. Top with cocoa powder.

Panettone French Toast
Soak Panettone in egg, brown sugar, cinnamon, and milk mixture. Butter skillet and cook about 2 minutes on each side until browned. Top with Cool Whip, fruit, and nuts.

Caramel Cinnamon Apple
Caramel pudding and apple pie filling. Add cinnamon to apple. Nuts optional. Top with powdered sugar and cinnamon.

Cool Whip Panettone Rollups
Cut a round slice of Panettone and roll it out flat. Spread Cool Whip and cinnamon. Nuts optional. Roll it up. Drizzle glaze on top. (See recipe above.)

OUR QUARANTINE KITCHENS

10

SALADS

Some have said they used everything
in the fridge to make their salads.

From the Quarantine Kitchen of
Jocelyn Hawkes

While I may not have the most amazing story, I am proud of the fact that I created this recipe from scratch! Being in quarantine the past few months, while unemployed, has been stressful and some days are harder than others. I can't always bring myself to cook but I was inspired to create something light and fresh on a very warm spring day.

Asian chicken salad! This was way better then expected! A homemade vinaigrette made this recipe delicious.

I decided to make something from scratch, just tasting as I go (except for the raw chicken!).

My kitchen, my sanctuary, the heart of my home.

INGREDIENTS

Chicken breasts (raw)

Mixed greens

Sliced almonds

Chow mein noodles

Mandarin orange slices

ASIAN CHICKEN SALAD

Marinate and refrigerate cut-up chicken breasts for minimum of 4 hours. You can do up to 24 hours.

Marinade
¼ cup soy sauce
2 teaspoons sesame oil
1 tablespoon honey
2 crushed garlic cloves
3-4 slices of fresh ginger root

When ready to cook, remove from marinade and heat a little oil in pan or put on a grill!

Garlic Ginger Vinaigrette
¼ cup olive oil
2 tablespoons (to start) low sodium soy sauce
2 minced garlic cloves
1-2 tablespoons honey (to taste)
1-2 tablespoons white wine vinegar (can also use rice wine vinegar)
1 tablespoon minced fresh ginger root
1 tablespoon toasted sesame oil

Taste and adjust as you go!

From the Quarantine Kitchen of
Regina Vicente

Our family loves homemade macaroni salad, and homemade deviled eggs, so I just began combining the two, and voilà, something everyone can enjoy!

INGREDIENTS

1 pound elbows (or pasta of choice)

1 cup mayo
(to start, can/will add more to taste)

½ cup sour cream
(to start, can add more)

1 teaspoon brown/spicy ground mustard (can add more)

½ teaspoon Adobo seasoning
(can add more)

¼ teaspoon salt
(optional)

½ to ¾ cup green olives
(can substitute)

3 - 5 hard boiled eggs,
sliced or chopped

½ finely diced onion
(yellow is our preference)

Dusting paprika, on top
(optional)

Deviled Egg Mac Salad

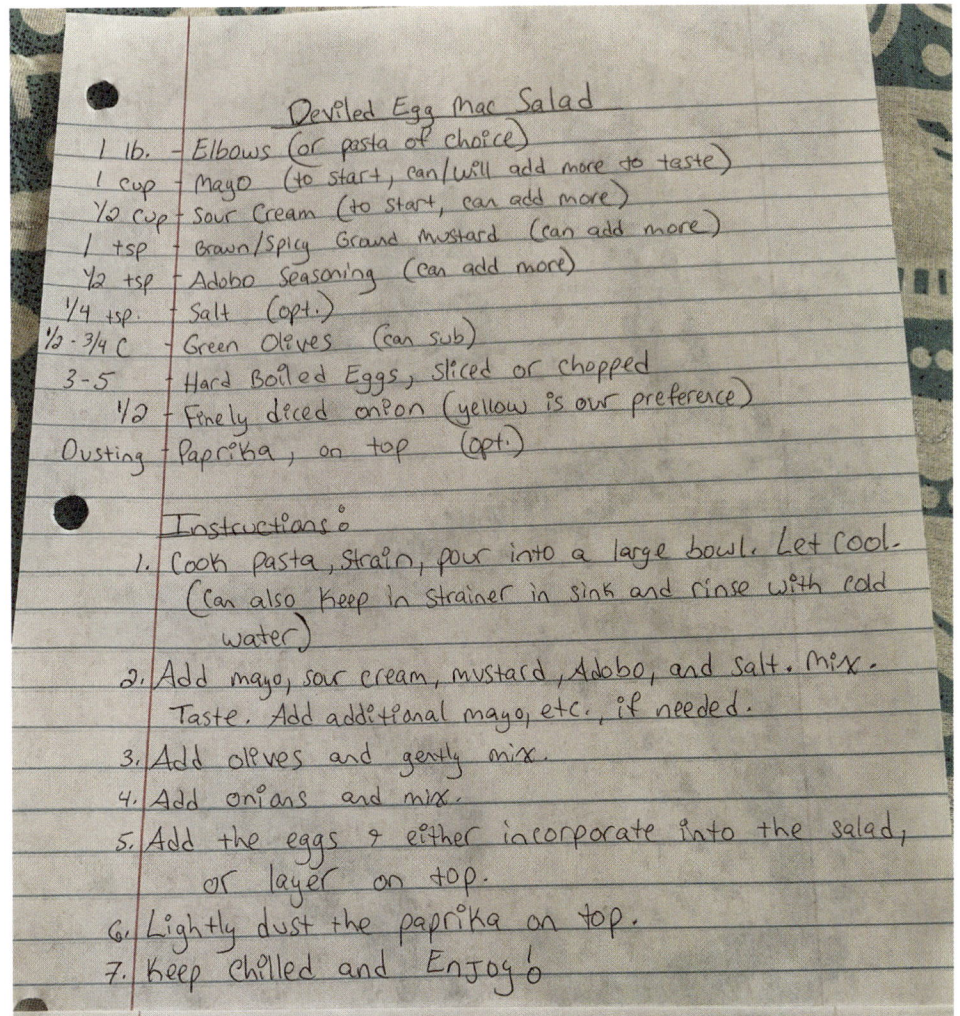

1 lb. - Elbows (or pasta of choice)
1 cup - Mayo (to start, can/will add more to taste)
½ cup - Sour Cream (to start, can add more)
1 tsp - Brown/Spicy Ground Mustard (can add more)
½ tsp - Adobo Seasoning (can add more)
¼ tsp. - Salt (opt.)
½ - ¾ C - Green Olives (can sub)
3 - 5 - Hard Boiled Eggs, sliced or chopped
½ - Finely diced onion (yellow is our preference)
Dusting - Paprika, on top (opt.)

Instructions:
1. Cook pasta, strain, pour into a large bowl. Let cool. (can also keep in strainer in sink and rinse with cold water)
2. Add mayo, sour cream, mustard, Adobo, and salt. Mix. Taste. Add additional mayo, etc., if needed.
3. Add olives and gently mix.
4. Add onions and mix.
5. Add the eggs & either incorporate into the salad, or layer on top.
6. Lightly dust the paprika on top.
7. Keep chilled and Enjoy!

INGREDIENTS

1 pound flat or string beans

2 potatoes

2 plum tomatoes

1 small red onion

2 cloves garlic

4 tablespoons extra virgin olive oil

2 tablespoons apple cider vinegar

Handful chopped basil

1 tablespoon oregano

Salt

Pepper

ITALIAN POTATO SALAD

Blanch 1 pound of flat beans or string beans.

Boil 2 potatoes whole (can use any potatoes, Yukon Gold potatoes pictured). After boiling, cube potatoes.

Cut up 2 plum tomatoes.

Cut up 1 small red onion.

Combine flat beans, potatoes, tomatoes, red onion and add 2 cloves of chopped garlic, 4 tablespoons of extra virgin olive oil, 2 tablespoons of apple cider vinegar, handful of chopped basil, 1 tablespoon oregano, salt and pepper to taste and then mix all ingredients together.

KATHLEEN'S
QUARANTINE KITCHEN
EST. 2020

From the Quarantine Kitchen of
Kathleen Russo

Hi! My name is Kathleen and I'm 36 years old, a native Staten Islander and the youngest of 5 kids from a big Italian family. I've been around food my whole life and quickly learned my way around the kitchen - thanks to my mom who is one of the best home chefs I know. I learned a lot from my maternal grandmother too; I'm certain I developed my own take on "no waste" because of her influence and the stories she told us about how they used everything because she grew up during the Great Depression. I know she would be so proud of me now; the way I can "cook the fridge" and make meals out of what most people would say is nothing. When this quarantine started, I didn't even go crazy stocking up on supplies, because I knew I could go at least 3 to 4 weeks with using what I had - just like Gramma would have done.

This summer salad was the great result of just throwing together ingredients I had on hand from the fridge and garden, and it totally works! Of course you can make your own adaptations; maybe mozzarella, black olives, and basil. Make it your own! Use what you have and enjoy the beautiful bounty we are blessed with.

SUMMER ORZO SALAD

INGREDIENTS

16 ounces orzo pasta

1 can garbanzo beans, drained

1 pint cherry tomatoes, sliced

1 cup kalamata olives, sliced

8 oz (or more) feta cheese, cubed or crumbled

1 bag/bunch fresh baby spinach, roughly chopped

½ cup pine nuts, toasted

Dressing:

2 lemons, juiced

½ cup olive oil

Large bunch fresh oregano, basil, and parsley, chopped finely

Salt and pepper to taste

Note: the amounts of dressing ingredients are suggestions; go by taste!

Boil the orzo as per the package directions; add a little oil to the water so it doesn't stick.

In the bottom of a large bowl, whisk together the dressing ingredients (oil, lemon juice, salt, pepper, and chopped fresh herbs).

Add the sliced tomatoes, olives, and drained beans to the bowl with dressing.

When the pasta is done, drain thoroughly and add to bowl. Toss to coat.

Gently fold in the chopped spinach and let the heat wilt it.

Add the feta cheese and toasted pine nuts.

Enjoy!

- Can be served warm, room temp, or cold.

- Leftovers can be stored in an airtight container and refrigerated for up to a week.

From the Quarantine Kitchen of
Jean Garcia

Growing up in an Italian-Filipino household, if you can imagine, there was always a lot going on in the kitchen. At age 10 I was inspired by my grandmother and father who taught me some great cooking skills. I would like to share a recipe of my own, eggplant caponata. Hope you enjoy it and as my grandmother would say Bon Appetit.

EGGPLANT CAPONATA

INGREDIENTS

½ cup of extra virgin olive oil (divided)

1 medium-sized onion (diced)

4 large garlic cloves (minced)

1 pint of sliced white mushrooms (or cremini)

(1) 14.5 oz. can of diced tomatoes

24 oz. can of tomato sauce (or three 8 oz. cans)

½ cup of black pitted olives (sliced)

2 large eggplants cut into half-inch slices then cut and cubed (skin on)

2 tablespoons of salt

1 tablespoon of black pepper

Pinch of crushed red pepper (optional)

¼ of a cup of fresh chopped parsley

Heat 2 tablespoons of olive oil over medium heat.

Add onion, cook until translucent for 30 seconds.

Stir in garlic for about 30 seconds until fragrant.

Combine mushrooms, diced tomatoes, and olives.

Add in 2 more tablespoons of olive oil and stir for about 2 minutes.

Combine eggplant and remaining olive oil.

Add in tomato sauce, salt, and pepper and stir occasionally until it comes to a boil.

Lower heat to simmer with the lid partially covered.

Continue to stir occasionally.

Cook time: about 60 minutes or until eggplant is fork-tender.

Garnish with chopped parsley.

Can serve with your favorite pasta, Italian bread, appetizer, side dish, or even over rice.

Salsa favorites from some of our members:

Roma tomatoes, garlic, red onion, cilantro, salt, fresh lime juice, splash of red wine vinegar and pulse in a food processor. You can add jalapeños for heat if you like.

Tomato, red and yellow peppers, onion, avocado, parsley, olive oil, salt, pepper, white balsamic glaze over crackers, add feta cheese if you wish.

1 avocado, 1 mango (pineapple works too) ½ bell pepper, ¼ seedless cucumber, ½ jalapeño (chopped fine), ¼ red onion, large handful of cilantro, ¼ teaspoon cumin, salt, juice of one lime. Cut all to desired size and mix.

Tomatoes, onion, lemon juice, salt, pepper, few drops of Louisiana Hot sauce, a drizzle of extra virgin olive oil, put in processor for a few seconds.

From the Quarantine Kitchen of
Chris Voltaggio

I found a passion for cooking at age 15 … 30 years later I'm still at it with an even greater passion. I was never professionally trained just learned and keep learning along the way.

My great grandfather was an amazing cook and I'm told he had the whole house smelling fantastic. Maybe I get it from him. My last name is Voltaggio and I often get asked if I'm related to the famous Voltaggio brother chefs, but, I don't believe I am. Either way, I just wanna make others happy with my food. So, enjoy!

CHRIS'S HOMEMADE SALSA

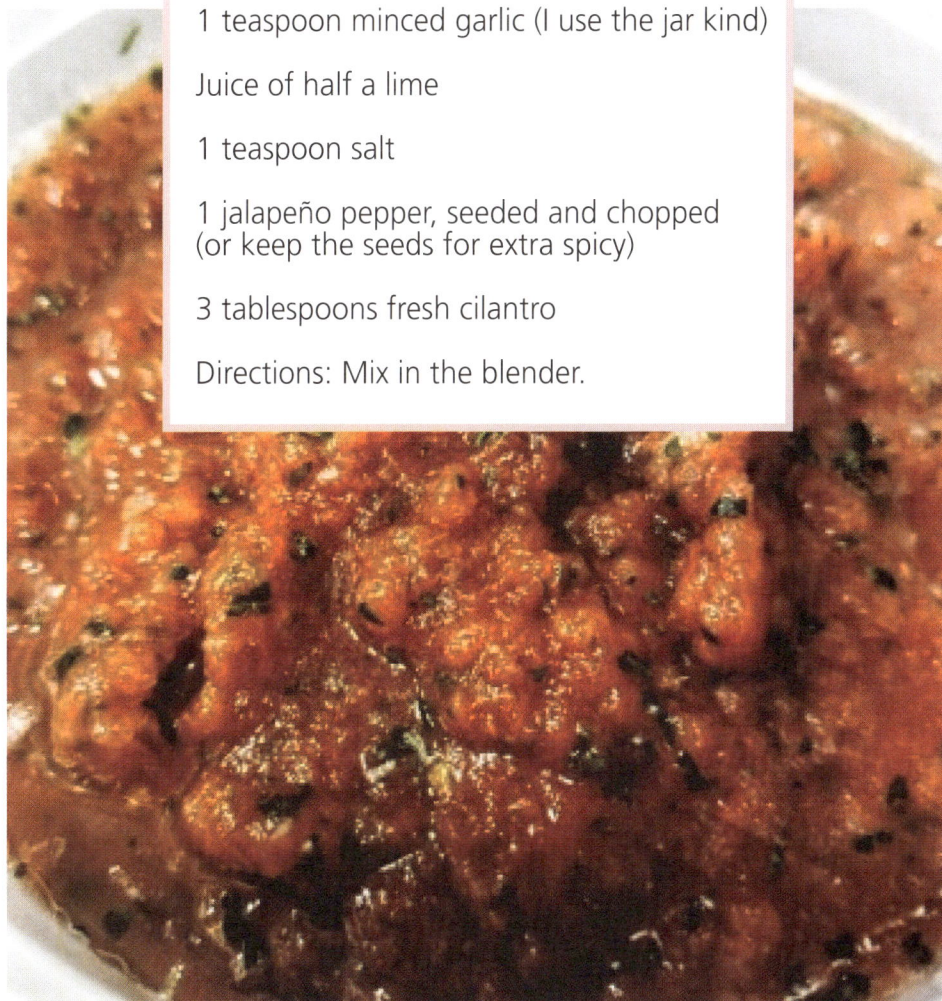

2 cans of Hunt's diced tomatoes, drained

Half of a red onion, chopped

1 teaspoon minced garlic (I use the jar kind)

Juice of half a lime

1 teaspoon salt

1 jalapeño pepper, seeded and chopped (or keep the seeds for extra spicy)

3 tablespoons fresh cilantro

Directions: Mix in the blender.

OUR QUARANTINE KITCHENS

BREADS

We tried our hand at bread.

From the Quarantine Kitchen of
Kristi Gregotowicz

This recipe was a party favorite that my god-mother Aunt Bunny would make all time! I would dream about it when I knew there was a party coming up. When Aunt Bunny passed away, I decided to keep the tradition alive and so I begin making it in her honor! I hope my Stromboli makes her proud!

I am born and raised American Italian from Staten Island, NY. I recently moved to South Carolina once my husband retired from the NYPD after 20 years of service and 10 years of owning a martial arts school called NY Finest Taekwondo. We decided on a simpler life down south as my daughter begins University of South Carolina this fall. She graduated in June of 2020 as valedictorian of her class. We are extremely proud of her and her future as a first responder nurse!

INGREDIENTS

Fresh pizza dough

½ pound of ham sliced thin

½ pound of salami sliced thin

½ pound of pepperoni sliced thin

One to two cups of mozzarella depending on how cheesy you like it

Olive oil

Garlic powder

STROMBOLI

Roll out pizza dough like a pizza pie.

Lay one layer of each topping (salami, ham, pepperoni, and shredded mozzarella); cold cuts should be sliced thin.

Roll stromboli tight and tuck in the ends.

Brush with olive oil and sprinkle generous amount of garlic powder along the top.

Bake at 350°F for 30 minutes.

Let cool a bit so it's easier to cut! Enjoy!

From the Quarantine Kitchen of
Rebecca Forman

I grew up eating this challah. My mother would make a batch and keep them in the freezer and we would have a loaf every Friday night. Since she grew up with her grandmother, my great-grand-mother, I always assumed it was a recipe passed down from Russia. It was only recently that I found out this recipe belonged to my aunt's college room-mate's family. So all these years thinking I'm channeling my ancestors, I'm really channeling someone else's ancestors.

No matter, because everyone who has ever tasted this challah proclaims it to be the best.

The woman whose recipe I thought this was until recently.

INGREDIENTS

8 cups flour

4 eggs, beaten

2 egg yolks

1 ⅓ cup sugar

2 sticks unsalted butter

2 cups lukewarm water

3 packages yeast

1 ½ teaspoon salt

CHALLAH BREAD

Mix water and yeast in medium sized bowl.

Sift flour, salt and sugar into large bowl.

Sift 3 cups of flour mixture into dissolved yeast bowl.
Stir until smooth. Cover and let sit for 30 minutes.

Meanwhile, cut butter into remaining flour mixture.

Add beaten eggs to yeast mixture, then add the yeast mixture
to the flour-butter bowl. Work together until not sticky, adding
more flour as necessary.

Knead at least ten minutes.

Turn into clean bowl, oil top. Cover and let rise two hours.

Knead dough again.

Form into challahs (braided loaves) place on greased
baking sheets. Cover and let rise one hour.

Brush loaves with egg yolks.

Bake at 350°F for 55 minutes.

Yield: 4 medium sized challah loaves.

In honor of my cousin Gregory Reda who lost his life on September 11. Gregory was born and raised and married his "endless love" Nicole on 4/28/95 in Brooklyn, NY.

To know him was to love him. His spirit continues to shine bright and his infectious smile and mannerisms live on in his two amazing sons.

Being Italian, Christmas Eve is a favorite holiday where family gathers and traditions (old and new) are embraced.

Scotcha was passed down from my grandmother to my mother and now to my siblings and I. Making scotcha is a wonderful family tradition that I hope will be passed on for many years to come.

When I remember my cousin Greg, I will always cherish the Christmas Eve's that we shared and the Scotcha that was enjoyed!

Scotcha

<u>Bread dough</u> - from local pizza store
if available or can buy frozen
in the store
  - cut each in 1/2 and roll out

<u>Filling</u>: Parsley
         Onions
         Provolone cheese — cut in cubes
         Marinara sauce (however you
         like to make it)

The amount of filling depends on how
many bread doughs you need to fill.
It is trial and error. I usually make
c 6 and have found that 2-3 bunches
of parsley and 2 bags of onions will
do. Cutting the onions is the worst part...
have learned through the years with
the help of technology that a chopper/
food processor is a lot easier.

All the ingredients get mixed together
in one bowl to make the filling.
Chop up parsley, cut onions and
Sautee in olive oil until soft, cut
provolone in cubes, salt and pepper
to taste and marinara sauce → mix
well in large bowl + taste.!

Now that the filling is ready, you
can start to fill the bread dough.
Place a scoop in the middle a spread
out along the length of the dough.
You don't want to overfill. Fold each
side of the dough over the filling and
tuck in the ends so the filling does
not leak out

Bake at 350° for @ 25 minutes or
until golden brown. Enjoy

From the Quarantine Kitchen of
Victoria and Isabella Garcia

Hi my name is Victoria Garcia. I'm 9 years old and I'm from Brooklyn, New York. I have a big family and a lot of siblings so we are always cooking a lot of food. My favorite part of the day is when my mom, my sister, and me wake up in the morning and go to the kitchen and make breakfast together. My mom always lets me have a taste before we sit down to eat as a family. I really love making different kinds of milkshakes. Setting the table is also fun to me because I can make it pretty. Besides cooking, I love gymnastics, swimming, making tik-toks and playing with my new puppy Nala. She's my best friend.

Hi my name is Isabella Garcia and I'm 9 years old and I'm from Brooklyn, New York. One thing you should know about me is that I really love to cook and bake. One of my favorite parts of my day is when my mom, me, and my sisters cook for everyone in my family. I love to cut up fruits and vegetables and I always get to help with the ingredients. I especially love baking cupcakes because I can make them colorful and they are my favorite sweet. Besides cooking and baking, I love to dance, do gymnastics, swim in my pool and make tik-toks.

Note from mom: *Thank you so much for allowing them to be a part of the cookbook. I told them the wonderful news and they are ecstatic. They believe they are now famous lol.* ♥

INGREDIENTS

Ingredients for dough:

¾ cup of extra virgin olive oil

2 ¼ cup teaspoons active dry yeast

2 ½ cups all purpose flour

1 cup warm water

3 garlic cloves, minced

½ teaspoon salt

¼ teaspoon pepper

½ teaspoon honey

Vegetables for your garden:

½ cup of baby spinach or fresh basil

5 cherry tomatoes, halved
(mix yellow and red)

2 thin slices of red onion

3 slices of baby bella mushrooms

¼ yellow pepper, sliced into
thin long pieces

8 asparagus spears

1-2 branches of fresh rosemary

GARDEN FOCACCIA

In a skillet add your olive oil, minced garlic, and black pepper. Cook on low heat, while stirring occasionally for about 3 minutes and set aside. You do not want to cook the garlic all the way, but instead only allow to flavor the oil.

In a medium-sized bowl, combine your warm water, honey, and yeast. Stir and let sit for 4 to 5 minutes.

Meanwhile add 1 ½ cups of your flour and ¼ cup of your garlic flavored olive oil to your bowl with honey and yeast. Stir and let sit for another 4 to 5 minutes.

Now, add the remaining flour and salt to your bowl. Mix until dough starts to form. Transfer to a floured surface and knead until it becomes smooth.

Lightly oil the inside of a large bowl. Place your dough inside and cover with a damp cloth and allow to rise for approximately 1 hour.

Once the hour has passed, preheat oven to 425°F. Add 1 tablespoon of your garlic flavored oil to coat the bottom of a baking sheet. Place your dough on your baking sheet. Then, with your fingertips start to lightly press down on the dough, creating round-like dimples.

Now, decorate your dough to create your garden by gently pressing down your asparagus, tomatoes, peppers, mushrooms, baby spinach, and fresh rosemary for the grass. Add the remainder of your oil and spread along the top of your dough, coating everything.

Bake for about 20 to 25 minutes or until golden.

Marrying into this family has been wonderful in so many ways. Sharing old family recipes and spending time together is what I love most. Time in quarantine has given me an opportunity to try these recipes, which I was once discouraged in making because I thought it was too hard. Turns out it wasn't and instead actually easy and rewarding. This recipe has been in this family since the 1920s and I am honored to be sharing it with you all.

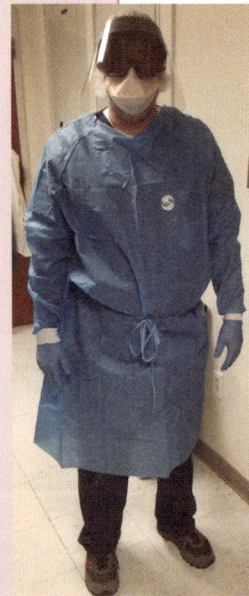

Below is a short message on the history of this bread by Aunt Ro, in memory of Grandma Rose Lifrieri.

Thank you to all front line healthcare workers! All essential workers! And most of all, God bless all!

A special thank you to my loving, supportive, amazing, and patient husband who is a front line emergency room healthcare worker: I LOVE YOU MATTHEW JOSEPH TRAYNOR!

My Mom's Sweet Bread Recipe

"I can remember helping my mom bake her sweet breads at Easter-time every year since I was 8 years old. I was her assistant. She told me to watch and learn. I would help her with all of the ingredients and she would stir and knead the dough. We left the dough in the pot where we mixed all the ingredients, covered it with a blanket, and finally let it rise in a dark place for 5 hours. Like magic, in 5 hours the dough was triple the size and we would make several breads. It was fun watching them bake and then later tasting what we created. We wrapped them when they were cool and gave them to family members and friends during the Easter season. My mom loved to cook, bake, and share with others. She was a wonderful mother and grandmother who loved her family. When she died, I was so touched that my nieces wanted her recipes that I shared. It was an honor to have my nieces make the sweet breads for my nephews and our family."

INGREDIENTS

Golden raisins (leave for last)

9 cups of all purpose flour

3 cups of sugar

A pinch or two of salt

9 eggs

3 sticks of butter

Dissolve the yeast in the lukewarm milk before adding to the rest of the ingredients.

6 ¾ teaspoons of dry active yeast (3 packages)

3 cups of milk

SWEET BREAD

In your main mixing bowl mix the flour, sugar, salt, eggs, and softened butter.

In a separate bowl, dissolve the yeast in lukewarm milk before adding it into the main bowl. Knead this consistently until it forms a dough. Add a cup or two of the golden raisins at this point to taste. (If the dough is still a little sticky add a few tablespoons of flour at a time.)

Once you have the dough, roll it into a ball and place it into the bowl.

Cover the bowl with cling wrap then place in a dark spot to rise (the key is to make sure the dough rests somewhere dark, I use a dark towel).

Wait 5 hours to let the dough rise.

After 5 hours, uncover the dough and cut 6 pieces before removing from the bowl.

Take the dough piece by piece out and form it into loaves that you will place on your baking sheet.

Bake for 1 hour at 300°F.

Enjoy!

From the Quarantine Kitchen of
Maria Monico

This is just a simple recipe but it has been my Easter tradition for more than 40 years. Everyone would call me Easter morning to see if I made the bread and come early and take some for breakfast and there would never be enough for our big Easter dinner! So I have since doubled the recipe. This year since we were quarantined my sisters Prudence and Lisa had to make it themselves. Hopefully next year will be back to normal.

My family loves it so much that I have made it numerous times since quarantined. This group has been so much fun I look forward to logging on to Facebook to see all the different recipes. Such a good diversion from all the crazy stuff going on in this world!

INGREDIENTS

1 cup milk

½ cup sugar

1 teaspoon salt

1 stick margarine

¼ cup warm water

2 packages yeast

1 tablespoon sugar

4 eggs

6 cups flour

EASTER BREAD

Heat together milk, sugar, salt, and margarine; set aside and let cool.

In a small cup, place warm water, yeast, and 1 tablespoon of sugar.

Meanwhile, beat eggs. Add to eggs, alternately, flour, milk mixture, and yeast mixture.

Knead a few minutes.

Place in a bowl; cover and let rise for 1 hour.

Divide dough in half and divide each half into thirds.

Form small portions into strips. Braid strips into a circle.

Cover and let rise 45 minutes.

Brush with beaten egg.

Bake 45 minutes at 325°F.

From the Quarantine Kitchen of
Ann Ariano

Spanakopita or Spinach Pie is a savory pastry that Greeks have been eating since ancient times. There are many variations of this famous dish. My favorite is the one created by my Yiayia, (Grandmother). Growing up in New Jersey, some of my most cherished memories are of sitting in her kitchen and watching her cook and bake. Yiayia Katina came to America from Greece as a young bride when she was only 18 years old. She left behind a large family in her native Crete. When she first arrived she had no idea how to cook! She wrote to her sisters who sent her family recipes and soon she became well known in her community as a wonderful cook. She loved preparing food for her family. Yiayia prepared her own phyllo for this recipe from scratch. While delicious, it is time consuming and can be tricky so my version uses good quality commercial phyllo that is readily available in grocery stores. Yiayia had this recipe in her head and never measured. One day a few years before she passed away, she showed me how to make it and I wrote down her recipe. I still bake it until (as she said in Greek) "it is nice and brown on top." The smell of it baking always reminds me of her. I love and miss you, Yiayia.

"... the world changed seemingly overnight when Covid-19 was declared a worldwide pandemic. My daughter's high school closed, my son came home from college, sports and activities were canceled. Suddenly everyone was home again and they were always hungry! With the extra time I planned out weekly menus that included family recipes and recipes from cookbooks that I finally had the time to read. We sat down together every night for dinner and lingered to talk and laugh. My family became my taste testers as I tried out new recipes and finally conquered my fear of baking bread. They waited patiently while I photographed my food and posted it on Facebook. I enjoyed sharing recipes and having foodie chats with Facebook friends and other members of the Quarantine Kitchen."

INGREDIENTS

10 sheets of commercial phyllo dough

8 oz. brick of cream cheese, softened

8oz. farmer's cheese (found near deli section of grocery stores)

½ cup extra virgin olive oil

2 large eggs

2 large bags fresh baby spinach, washed, dried, and roughly chopped

1 ½ sticks butter melted (to brush on the sheets of phyllo dough)

Salt and pepper

Optional add ins:
(My father added these to my grandmother's recipe when he put it on the menu at his NYC Greek restaurant in the early 1980s)

¼ crumbled feta

2 more eggs

2 scallions or 1 leek, chopped fine

2 small yellow onions, chopped fine

YIAYIA'S SPANAKOPITA

Preheat oven to 350°F.

Combine spinach, softened cream cheese, farmer's cheese, eggs, and olive oil in large bowl. Add salt and pepper.

Open the phyllo box after you have combined the other ingredients and melted your butter (1 ½ sticks).

Layer 5 sheets of phyllo in the bottom of a baking dish; brush each sheet with melted butter; tuck in edges of phyllo.

Add spinach/cheese mixture to the pan. Top with 5 additional sheets of phyllo, brushing each sheet with melted butter. Make sure to brush the top sheet too.

Score with a knife (at least 2 parallel lines or into serving pieces - it's easier to cut later if you do this.)

Sprinkle top of the pie with a few drops of water before putting it in the oven.

Bake at 350°F for approximately 45 to 55 minutes. You will start to smell it cooking - keep checking. When the top is a nice golden brown it's done (refer to my picture).

Let cool about 10 minutes before serving. Serves: 8 to 12.

Recipe Notes: If you are not serving the spanakopita immediately do not cover it because the phyllo will get soggy. Let it cool completely before covering (it's best served hot from the oven). Reheat leftovers in the oven. Microwave will make the phyllo soggy. Phyllo can be tricky to work with. You need to work quickly so it doesn't dry out. You may want to cover it with a damp towel as you work. The pie can be baked in a rectangular or circular pan. You can also make it into phyllo triangles. Lay out two pieces of phyllo dough, cut them in half lengthwise, brush with butter. Put a spoonful of mixture on one end and fold into a triangle, brush triangle with more butter. This recipe will make approximately 25 triangles. The triangles can be baked immediately or frozen for later use. It's fine to bake them from frozen but they will take longer to cook.

From the Quarantine Kitchen of
Jocelyn Hawkes

I have a little bit of a sentimental tidbit to add:

The honey I used in this loaf inspired the recipe.

My dad was a hobby beekeeper and had a few hives he tended to right up until his passing. I have a stash of his honey that was harvested by a local beekeeper my mom brought in, so his hard work wouldn't go to waste. There is nothing like organic honey created with love.

Tell your parents you love them!

And support your local beekeepers!

INGREDIENTS

1 ½ teaspoons of active dry yeast

3 to 3 ½ cups flour (you can use white all purpose or 1 cup wheat, plus 2 to 2 ½ cups white)

3 tablespoons of your favorite flavor honey or plain. About 2 teaspoons less if you don't want a very sweet bread

½ teaspoon salt

2 tablespoons + 2 teaspoons vegetable oil

1 cup warm water for proofing

HONEY LOAF BREAD

Preheat oven to 375°F.

Dissolve yeast in warm water, then add honey and stir.
Add 1 cup flour, salt and oil, then work in remainder of flour gradually.

Knead for 10 to 15 minutes until smooth and elastic.

Put in a well-oiled bowl, cover with a warm damp towel, free from draft.

Let rise for about 45 minutes or until doubled in bulk.

Punch down, shape into loaf, and put in a well-oiled loaf pan.

Let it rise again until it's about an inch to an inch and a half above the top of the pan. It could take an hour, could take longer. Let it rise for that nice sandwich bread look.

Bake for 25 to 30 minutes, until golden brown.

You really should wait until it's completely cool before cutting into it so it doesn't get soggy. But it's very difficult to wait sometimes.

This bread fed us when we couldn't get to the store for several weeks at the start of the quarantine. It keeps, but it won't last for long, it's too good!

Toast it up for a nice sandwich, slice it thick for French toast, or just have a slice with your favorite jam.

LISA'S TURKEY SPECIAL

From the Quarantine Kitchen of
Lisa Corazza

INGREDIENTS

4 long Ciabatta rolls

Canned chipotle peppers

½ cup mayonnaise

1 pound bacon

1 ½ pounds deli turkey (sliced thin)

¼ pound sliced provolone cheese

2 bundles collard greens

1 clove garlic

Salt and pepper

Fry the 1 pound of bacon, putting aside 4 slices for collards.

While bacon is frying, clean, strip, and chop collard greens.

Drain off about half of the bacon grease from the pan. Press or finely chop garlic, add to bacon grease pan. (Careful not to brown the garlic.) Rinse collards and put in pan with garlic. Add salt and pepper to taste. Allow to cook and wilt down, stirring occasionally, about 20 minutes. Dice the 4 slices of bacon (small) and add to collard greens. Continue with a small flame under collards for about 10 to15 minutes, stirring occasionally.

I make my own chipotle mayo using 1 chipotle pepper, canned (chopped fine), some of the liquid from the can, and approximately ½ cup of mayonnaise.

Assemble your sandwiches:

Slice ciabatta rolls lengthwise. Drop turkey deli-style to fill each roll. Put a heaping serving spoon of the collard mixture on each, 3 slices of bacon, and cover with provolone slices. Spread chipotle mayo on the inside of the top of the roll and top of the sandwich. Heat a grill pan on the stove. Lightly butter top of the sandwich and put face down on grill pan. Press with food press and toast until crisp. Butter underside of sandwich and flip in the pan. Press and toast until crisp.

IRISH SODA BREAD

This soda bread is an old recipe that I've used for years. It is a bit cake-like and moister than traditional soda bread.

I like to make them around St. Patrick's Day, but they usually appear more than that over the year.

INGREDIENTS

3 ½ cups all-purpose flour

⅔ cup sugar

2 teaspoons baking powder

½ teaspoons baking soda

1 teaspoon salt

1 pint sour cream

2 eggs

1 teaspoon vanilla

¾ cup dark raisins

2 tablespoons caraway seeds (optional)

Preheat oven to 350°F.

Combine all dry ingredients into a bowl and set aside.

In a separate bowl or stand mixer, beat sour cream, eggs, and vanilla.

With mixer on low, add dry ingredients until just combined (do not over mix). Fold in caraway seeds if using. The batter will be very sticky.

Spray 9-inch springform with baking spray and add batter. Wet your hands slightly to form it into place.

Cut a cross into the top of bread and dust lightly with flour.

Bake for 48 to 50 minutes. The toothpick will come out dry when done.

Cool on wire rack for 30 minutes.

OUR QUARANTINE KITCHENS

APPETIZERS

Random things we made during quarantine that we wouldn't normally make ... and we ate it all.

From the Quarantine Kitchen of
Francine Ingrassia

When I was growing up, cooking and mealtimes around the table were a way for us to stay close as a family. As a matter of fact, I don't recall a time that my parents ever ordered in. With our large Italian family of eight, it was unheard of. My dad, Carmelo, was born in Licata, Sicily. Cooking to him was so natural. He imbued us with his Sicilian style in our Brooklyn home. As the proud owner of Valoroso Construction in Carroll Gardens, New York, he restored brownstones back to their original grandeur. Once home, he would jump in the shower and rush to start cooking his incredible meals with my loving mother, Camilla, an evening ritual they both loved.

My entire family would gather in the kitchen, once they smelled the fresh ingredients wafting on the stove and in the oven. The secret to their master recipes was that they only used fresh foods. Going to the local market was also a beloved daily ritual, where they would pick their favorite items. Neighbors knew my parents for not only their tremendous, generous hearts, but also for their Sicilian culinary works of art that my parents shared with them. My father loved to feed the neighbors.

INGREDIENTS

6 large or 8 medium-sized artichokes, cleaned and trimmed

2 lemons

¾ cup of olive oil

Salt, to taste

Pepper, to taste

8 garlic cloves, chopped

1 cup of fresh parsley, chopped and rinsed (set aside a little to garnish each artichoke after placing in crock pot)

1 cup of Pecorino Romano cheese

6 tomatoes diced, rinsed

2 containers of College Inn chicken broth

1 small container of 4C seasoned breadcrumbs (it comes in two sizes)

Important to use fresh garlic and fresh parsley, they are delicious when fresh ingredients are used. Do not substitute.

SICILIAN STUFFED ARTICHOKES

Rinse your artichokes under cold water. Pat dry with a clean kitchen towel or paper towel. Remove any stray leaves from the stems of the artichokes.

With kitchen shears or sharp scissors, remove the thorny tips from the leaves.

With a sharp chef's knife or serrated knife, cut about an inch off the top of the artichokes.

Keep a lemon handy to rub onto the exposed areas of the artichoke so they do not oxidize and turn brown. They will oxidize if you skip this step.

Remove the bitter, fibrous end of the stem with your sharp knife, leaving about an inch left on the artichoke. Be sure to rub a lemon on the exposed part of the stem.

After you are done cleaning and trimming the artichokes, squeeze the lemons in an 8-quart pot with water. Place artichokes in this bath upside down; you can use a plate to keep them in the water for 15 minutes. The lemon will tenderize the leaves. After 15 minutes, remove and rinse. Let them dry upside down for 5 minutes. Dry with a towel.

To stuff: Combine fresh chopped garlic, fresh chopped parsley, salt, pepper, Pecorino Romano cheese, and breadcrumbs. Mix well. Drizzle olive oil in the mixture. It should be damp, not soaked.

Stuff each artichoke with the mixture using a spoon. Make sure you open them to evenly spread the mixture inside. Pat stuffing down inside the artichoke.

Place artichokes in a crockpot (they should fit tightly). I can get 6 large ones or 8 small ones in my large oval crockpot. Garnish tops of artichokes with parsley.

Carefully fill the crockpot with the two containers of chicken broth. Fill to about ¾ the way up the artichoke. Cover the pot.

Turn crockpot on high for 6 to 7 hours. Add tomatoes to the broth around the 3rd hour. Do not open the pot often because it will release the heat.

Once you can put a knife straight through the center of the artichoke, it is ready. Be careful to make sure liquid is covering ¾ of the artichoke. If not, add some more. After cooking for hours, some of the liquid might have to be replenished.

Serve in individual bowls with some broth and tomatoes. Buon Appetito!

Artichokes are actually flowerings that haven't blossomed. Historians believe the artichoke originated in the Mediterranean countries, possibly Sicily.

My father and mother would prepare 20 to 30 artichokes at a time. They flew off the table when we were growing up. No one left the table without devouring them! My dad was staying with me for a few days and wanted me to take him to Brooklyn to buy artichokes because you can get them at a produce stand for so much less. I tried to explain to him that the time and gas with my SUV would not be worth it; his disappointment was apparent. So I took the trip from Garden City, Long Island to Brooklyn so he can savor the moment of his hometown. It was a favorite spot of his to visit and he loved playing some bocce with his friends so, of course, we stopped at the park. He must have bought 50 artichokes that day and I'm not kidding, prepared them all in one sitting.

During this uncertain time, with a growing family of mostly teens quarantined in their rooms to study and, well, of course–sleep throughout the days–the only time I was seeing my growing family was when we gathered together at the kitchen table for our family dinner. Garlic, the star condiment in my kitchen, plays a leading role. The aroma draws them in. It is a flavor powerhouse that adds a lot of benefits to your food. So, when I use it, suddenly every-one appears from their quarantined quarters for a stroll downstairs to see "what's cookin'?" It's quite amusing to watch it unfold.

The Quarantine Kitchen Facebook group has brought my family together in exactly the same way my father and mother brought me and my siblings, decades ago, when we didn't have chaotic busy schedules like today. My graduating daughter has found a new passion in the kitchen and it is bringing us closer together in another way. Even my boys are helping to cook with me. As a mother of a 2020 high school graduate, it has been a wonderful way for us to come together and talk about the silver linings that this pandemic has brought. It has been a blessing spending this time with my family that I might not ordinarily have had. While my daughter may not have had the rest of her senior year to complete, other memories were made for posterity.

The end is not always the end but the start of a new beginning.

During these uncertain times in this global health crisis, we realize we cannot control its circumstances, but we have become a stronger, more loving and compassionate family, despite our individual quarantine challenges. We are all facing them together and our dinners are where we convey how grateful we are to have each other to lean on.

My heart hurts that my daughter, Jules, has lost so much of her senior year in high school but we are together as a family and are finding gratitude in our hearts for the moments we share and the memories we are making with each and every meal.

RECIPE

Dish: Rice Balls   Serves: 15 pieces

- 1 Tablespoon Olive Oil
- 1 small onion chopped
- 1 clove garlic crushed
- 1 cup uncooked Arborio Rice
- 1/2 cup dry white wine
- 2 1/2 cups boiling Chicken stock
- Salt & pepper to taste
- 1/2 cup grated cheese

- 1 egg beaten
- 1 egg
- 1 tablespoon Milk
- 4oz cubed mozzarella
- 1/2 cup flour
- 1 cup breadcrumbs
- oil for deep frying

Heat olive oil over medium heat. Add onion & garlic until soft. Pour in rice and stir

for 2 minutes stir in wine and cook until liquid is evaporated. Add hot chicken stock a little at a time until evaporated before adding more. Season with salt & pepper. Turn off heat and add cheese.

Transfer risotto to a bowl and allow to cool about 20 minutes. Beat egg & stir into risotto. In a seperate bowl wisk together egg & milk. For each ball roll 2 tablespoons of risotto into a ball peace a piece of mozzarella into middle roll into a ball. Coat with flour egg & breadcrumbs. FRY & EAT

Calories _____
Cholesterol _____
Sodium _____

Source: _____

Another quality product from LABEL&co P.O. Box 223, Baldwin, NY 11510

ZUCCHINI PIE

From the Quarantine Kitchen of
Allison Marchese-Cararo

Peel zucchini and slice it thin. Put to the side.

In a bowl add Bisquik, eggs, oil, cheese, salt, and pepper.

Cut up a little bit of scallion. I use one scallion (If you only have onion that's fine. But scallions are a bit milder. I don't use much but if you like onion add to your liking.)

Cut up some mozzarella in small small pieces and/or American cheese.

Mix all together.

Bake at 350°F for about 45 minutes.

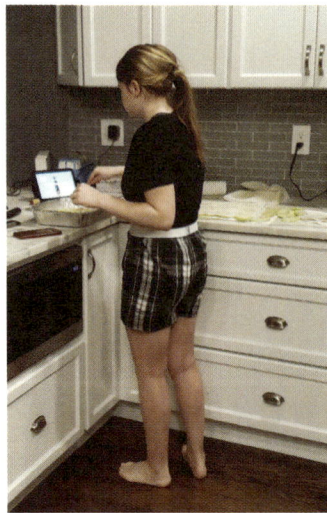

INGREDIENTS

3 cups zucchini

1 cup Bisquik

5 eggs

½ cup of oil

½ cup grated cheese

Salt

Pepper

1 scallion

Mozzarella or American cheese

MARTARELLA'S PANELLE

INGREDIENTS

**1 ½ cups chickpea flour
(Bob's Red Mill Garbanzo)**

3 cups water

**1 teaspoon coarse fresh salt
or kosher salt**

2 tablespoons chopped fresh parsley

Canola oil

Pour the chickpea flour, water, and salt in a medium-sized saucepan and whisk until smooth. Set over medium heat and whisk constantly as the mixture slowly heats. Cook and keep whisking, scraping the bottom and sides of the pan frequently, until the mixture is smooth, thick, and starts to pull away from the sides of the pan, about 5 minutes. Remove from heat and stir in the parsley.

Pour the mixture onto a cold, clean baking sheet (approximately 12"x15") and spread it quickly with a spatula, before it cools and sets, so it fills the pan in an even layer, about ¼ inch thick. Let cool in the refrigerator an hour, until completely firm.

Once cooled, cut into squares with a sharp knife. Carefully lift the cut pieces from the pan.

To fry the panelle, pour enough canola oil into a wide heavy skillet to cover the bottom, to a depth of ½ inch, and set over medium heat. When the oil is hot, fry the panelle about 3 minutes, until underside is gold, then flip and brown the other side. Place panelle on paper towels to drain excess oil. Drizzle lightly with salt and serve hot. The panelle may be served on a fresh roll with ricotta and grated parmesan cheese.

From the Quarantine Kitchen of
Laura Caroccia

Growing up in the 60s, as the third generation in an all-Italian household, in an all-Italian neighborhood, I thought everyone on the planet ate fried meatballs for breakfast on Sunday mornings. Even my classmates were all like me ... we called Sunday's dinner "Sunday's Macaroni and Meatballs with Gravy" and everyone had at least one female relative who wore only black with her nylon stockings rolled down under her knees. We grew up with the sounds of Caruso and Sinatra. Tomatoes, eggplants, and peppers and every other conceivable vegetable, herb, and the mandatory fig trees were planted in backyards and front yards too. Years later, I can still recall how the fig trees, dressed for winter in their burlap wraps with large tin pails on the top reminded me of sentries at a lonely outpost. Only the rich, or the lazy, had lawns instead of vegetable gardens. And we felt sorry for them.

I learned this recipe and so many more from my Grandma Paolina Malgioglio Leone. What an amazing woman she was! Born in 1898, she and her younger sister came to America, alone, when she was just 17. By 1917 she was married and by 1922 she had 2 children of her own and became the primary caregiver of her husband's 3 young nieces, their mother passing from the flu epidemic that decimated the lower East Side of New York and most of America.

She so reminds me of the resiliency of all those women who came before us ... how they lived through pandemics and wars and the Great Depression and, thanks to strong family and strong faith, for the most part emerged happy and whole. Happy and whole. It's what I wish for all of us as we share our friendship and our love of cooking in our Quarantine Kitchens.

INGREDIENTS

2 large green bell peppers

½ cup white rice

1 medium onion (about ¾ cup) coarsely chopped

¾ to 1 pound ground sirloin

¼ cup raisins

3 thin slices Genoa salami or prosciutto (cut into small pieces)

1 sundried tomato coarsely chopped

1 teaspoon minced parsley

¼ cup pignoli nuts

¼ - ½ cup grated Pecorino Romano cheese

Salt and pepper

1 cup "simple" tomato sauce

Olive oil

STUFFED PEPPERS

Wash 2 large, green, bell peppers and remove ½ inch off the top and put aside. Discard the pith and seeds.

Prepare ½ cup white rice according to package directions and set aside.

Heat ¼ to ½ cup olive oil (or a combination of olive oil and butter) in a large skillet. Add the onion and sauté until very tender. Crumble in the chopped meat and cook over low flame until there is no more pink. Add the raisins and sundried tomato. Stir to blend.

Add in 1 teaspoon salt and ¼ teaspoon ground black pepper. Stir in the parsley, pignoli nuts, and the salami. Simmer for a minute and add in the cooked rice. Mix well. Remove from heat and stir in the grated cheese. Taste and adjust seasonings if necessary. Add ¼ cup of the simple tomato sauce to the mixture just to moisten it.

Generously fill (and pack down the filling in) the pepper bottoms, mounding in center and cover with the reserved top. Place in a shallow baking dish.

Pour the remaining sauce over all. Add ¼ cup water to the baking dish and drizzle with olive oil. Cover and bake in a preheated 350°F oven for 50 to 70 minutes or until the pepper shells are fork tender. Note: If you have more stuffing than will fit in the pepper just add it to the tomato sauce in the baking dish. MANGIA BENE!

The decidedly Sicilian addition of raisins and pignoli nuts to the stuffing, make this dish equally delicious as an entrée or served without the pepper but with lots of crusty Italian bread in what we called a Sloppy Giuseppe (my Grandma Leone's version of a Sloppy Joe).

STUFFED PORTOBELLO MUSHROOMS

INGREDIENTS

4 Portobello mushrooms

1 pound of lean ground turkey

1 bag of fresh baby spinach

½ cup - ¾ cup fresh mozzarella, cut into small pieces

Garlic powder

Onion powder

Parsley

Crushed red pepper flakes

1-2 tablespoons olive oil

About a ¼ cup of white wine

Cook turkey meat in olive oil until it doesn't look pink any longer. Add garlic and onion powder, salt, parsley, and red pepper flakes. Mix well, cook for about 5 minutes. Add wine, cook on high flame and let it come to a boil, then simmer. Add spinach and cover until it wilts.

Place portobello mushrooms in a baking pan. Add all the ingredients into each mushroom. Lastly, top with mozzarella and cook in oven for about 30 minutes at 350°F, covered. After 30 minutes, uncover and place back in the oven for about another 5 to10 minutes until done.

Buon Appetito!

From the Quarantine Kitchen of
Carmela Sostenuto

My family has a passion for cooking. One of our traditional Christmas dish is a stuffed potato pie called gattó.

We never have any written recipes because we learned by watching my grandmother and mother.

This is one of our family's favorite. It's our traditional dish we must have for Thanksgiving, Christmas, and Easter. Or, just because we enjoy yummy food.

INGREDIENTS

5 pounds russet potatoes

3 hard-boiled eggs, thin sliced

6 oz. fresh mozzarella, thin sliced

½ pound ham, thin slices

1 tablespoon grated Romano cheese

For the potato mixture:

8 eggs

¾ cup bread crumbs

1 cup grated Pecorino Romano

½ teaspoon black pepper

1 teaspoon salt

¼ teaspoon baking soda

For the beef & sauce:

4 minced garlic cloves

1 small chopped onion

1 ½ pounds ground beef

(1) 6 oz. tomato paste + 6 oz. water

1 tablespoon grated Romano

Fresh chopped basil

POTATO PIE (GATTÓ DI PATATE)

Boil the potatoes until a knife goes through easily. Mash the potatoes and store in the fridge for a few hours. I usually do this the day before.

Sauté garlic and onions in olive oil for about 5 minutes, or until onions are tender. Add the ground beef and cook for 5 to 6 minutes. Add peas (optional) and cook for another 5 minutes. Add tomato paste, water, salt, and black pepper until cooked (approximately 12-15 minutes). Add 1 table-spoon of grated Romano and set aside.

Mix potatoes, bread crumbs, cheese, salt, pepper, baking soda, and eggs. Mix well until the potato mixture is soft.

I use an 11 inch round pan, 2 inches deep. Grease with olive oil. Take a bit of potato mixture and flatten it with my hands, about ¼ inch thick and cover the pan and sides. I put a little water on my hands so it is easier to handle the mixture. Drizzle a tiny bit of olive oil and smooth it so there are no holes.

Add a layer of ham, a thick layer of ground beef, some grated cheese, fresh mozzarella, and hard-boiled eggs. Add another layer of ham on top.

Now, cover the entire pie with the rest of the potato mixture. Flatten it as you did before. Drizzle olive oil and smooth the top and sides so it is nice and sealed.

Cook it on the stove, a very low flame, for about 20 minutes. Make sure it is not sticking by shaking the pan every 5 minutes. Once you see it's nice and light brown, put it in the oven to cook the top at 350°F for 30 minutes, or until golden brown. Once golden brown, broil for 5 minutes. I have always used a regular frying pan for this, I just remove the handle.

Let it cool off for 10 minutes. Put a plate over the top of the pie and flip it over, or just slice inside the pan.

My mother would flip it and finish cooking it on the stove. I find it much easier to stick it in the oven. Enjoy it!

From the Quarantine Kitchen of
Ryan Lewis

This is a traditional, hearty comfort food with a twist. The meatiness of traditional chili is created by combining shredded beets and grainy red quinoa, which gives nice texture, subtle sweetness and nuttiness to this delicious dish. The feedback on this dish has been amazing across the board, and I hope you love it as well!

Pre-prep: 5 to10 minutes
Cook time: 15 to 20 minutes
Total: 20 to 30 minutes
Serves: 4 to 6 people

INGREDIENTS

3 cups cooked red quinoa

½ cup vegetable broth

1 clove garlic

¼ jalapeño pepper (or to taste)

1 medium onion

1 medium beet

1 medium bell pepper

24 oz. jar strained tomatoes

15 oz. can pinto beans

15 oz. can kidney beans

15 oz. can black beans

1 tablespoon paprika

1 teaspoon cumin

1 teaspoon oregano

1 teaspoon salt

1 teaspoon black pepper

BEAN & BEET CHILI

During the cooking process, add splashes of broth when things start to dry, and stir frequently.

Mince garlic and begin to simmer over medium heat in the base of a medium pot or sauce pan with splashes of vegetable broth. Add minced jalapeño, if desired.

Once garlic begins to release aroma, after 2 minutes or so, add chopped onion, grated beet, chopped bell pepper and dry seasonings. Cover and steam-sauté about 8 minutes, or until cooked to your liking.

Add strained tomato, and pre-cooked beans. Bring to a simmer, and allow ingredients to cook and flavors to meld to your liking, anywhere from 5 to 30 minutes, or beyond. But as soon as all ingredients are warmed through, it can be ready.

Cooked red quinoa can be mixed in, or alternatively serve chili over the quinoa.

Suggestions:

- Substitute the beans in this dish with 1 or multiple others.

- Top with cilantro leaves, or avocado.

- Other quinoas or other cooked grains work well also, such as brown rice, millet, or even cornmeal polenta.

From the Quarantine Kitchen of
Alexa Wyman

This recipe is a definite go-to for me and my family. Just about everyone I serve it to loves it. We usually eat it as mac and cheese, but it's also great for dipping or loaded nachos, or on steamed broccoli or other vegetables. So easy too! It keeps in the fridge for 3 to 5 days or more.

Pre-prep: 10 minutes
Cook time: 10 to12 minutes
Total: 20 to 30 minutes
Serves: 4 to 6 people

CASHEW CHEESE SAUCE

INGREDIENTS

In order of appearance:

16 oz. pasta of choice (elbows, spirals, shells, penne work well)

1 to 2 carrots

1 small onion

1 ½ cup broth or water

1 ½ cup cashews

2 to 3 garlic cloves

¼ cup nutritional yeast

¼ teaspoon salt

Dash of cayenne

½ tablespoon turmeric powder

½ cup milk of choice
(we usually use almond)

1 tablespoon lemon juice

2 teaspoon mustard

Boil a large pot of water for pasta. Once boiling, add pasta and cook.

In a smaller pot, boil chopped carrots and onion in water or broth until veggies are tender. Reserve cooking liquid.

Add cashews, garlic cloves, nutritional yeast, salt, cayenne, turmeric powder, vegetables, and still hot cooking liquid to the blender. Let it soak for a few minutes.

Add milk of choice, lemon juice and mustard to the blender and blend on high until smooth.

Add the boiled carrots and onion with cooking liquid to blender and blend on high until it becomes a smooth consistency.

Pour cheese over pasta, vegetables, nachos, whatever you fancy really.

Suggestions:

- Any milk seems to work - in the past I've use almond, macadamia, coconut, and hemp.

- We love high-protein pastas such as those made with lentil, chickpea, beans, green peas, etc. They may soak up more sauce than you're used to so add extra if need be. They are a great option though for gluten-free, low-glycemic, paleo/keto, etc.

From the Quarantine Kitchen of
Ryan Lewis & Alexa Wyman

This recipe combines each of our star recipes into one crowd-pleasing dish! We like to focus on the quality of the chili and cheese, and then make the assembly of the nachos simple on ourselves. You can make it way more extravagant than we do with the toppings.

Pre-prep: 30 minutes
Cook time: 5 minutes
Total: 30 to 40 minutes
Serves: 4 to 6 people

INGREDIENTS

In order of appearance:

Large bag tortilla chips

2 cups Bean & Beet Chili (page 59)

2 cups Cashew Cheesesauce (page 61)

Small jar pickled jalapeños

LOADED CHILI & CHEESE NACHOS

Work in layers:

Fill a large plate with chips without too much stacking.

Pour or spoon a layer of chili.

Pour or spoon a layer of cheese sauce.

Sprinkle some pickled jalapeños around.

Repeat until the plate is as large as you desire.

Suggestions:

We gave the basic recipe, but you can take this as far as you want. Some good additions are sliced black olives, salsa or salsa verde, avocado, green onion, cilantro, lime juice, sour cream, chopped tomatoes or pico de gallo, and hot sauce.

GREAT GRANDMA EVELYN'S KNISH

INGREDIENTS

Dough:

2 ½ cups flour

2 tablespoons olive oil

2 tablespoons white vinegar

1 cup water

1 ½ teaspoons kosher salt

1 egg

Filling:

2 ½ to 3 pounds russet potatoes

2 large onions, chopped finely

4 to 6 tablespoons of oil

2 tablespoons butter

Mix (I add ½ cup of flour at a time) and knead ingredients as you would a pie crust. You know you have enough flour when the dough isn't sticky.

Wrap the dough in plastic wrap and refrigerate for an hour.

Boil potatoes for 15 to 20 minutes; drain and cool for 5 to 10 minutes (this is important). Cook chopped onions in oil, until caramelized.

Mash potatoes, but leave a bit rough (not as smooth as mashed potatoes); add cooked onions and butter and mix well with hands.

Roll the dough out thin, on parchment paper or a mat.

Cut into slices or cut out rounds about 2 ½ inches wide.

Take as much filling as you like rolled by hand, and put on dough; wrap dough around filling. The dough stretches easily without breaking. Roll until that piece of dough completely covers the filling.

Use an egg wash (slightly beaten egg with some water), to brush on top of each knish.

Bake on a cookie sheet (you can line with parchment paper) at 375°F for 35 to 40 minutes, until the top browns.

Enjoy!

From the Quarantine Kitchen of
Trevor Manning

In February, we adopted a medium-sized dog, Mimi. I am a respiratory therapy student, and Kerry is a high school science teacher. When quarantine started, we needed to make some quick moves to prepare for school from home. First, we put new carpet and desks in our loft. Being newly rescued, Mimi wanted to be with us at all times and would bark non stop when we climbed the ladder to "go to work." So we built her a staircase. We turned a dirty sunroom that was used for storage by the previous homeowners into our favorite room to spend a rainstorm with floors we put in ourselves and the furniture that we handmade. We spent countless time working on countless projects, but one thing was always the same: Trevor loved experimenting with recipes and different styles of cooking. Please enjoy this grilled wing recipe. Hopefully, it won't be long before you can cook it for friends and family!

I want to dedicate this recipe to my parents Thomas and Cheryl Manning. Both of my parents are retired nurses and have a combined nursing and health care experience of over 60 years. They have touched and saved countless lives over their respected careers and I am grateful and honored to be their son.

INGREDIENTS

2 pounds of fresh chicken wings

(2) 12 oz cans of beer (I use a local, fruity, "crushable" IPA style beer here in NJ)

1 tablespoon of smoked salt (I use Maldon salt) or any quality sea salt

1 tablespoon fresh cracked black pepper

3-4 cloves of fresh GRATED garlic (grating your garlic is easier than chopping)

1-2 inch knob of fresh ginger GRATED (use the back of a soup spoon to easily peel ginger)

1-2 shallots chopped (shallots don't grate well and become to liquidy)

Zest and juice from half an orange

Zest and juice from 1 lemon

1-2 tablespoons of pickle juice (I only use juice from half-sour pickles but feel free to change it up)

FRESH DILL- This is why I love this recipe. See NOTE.

BEER SOAKED GRILLED WINGS

Step 1 - Dry your wings using paper towels to make sure the seasonings will stick and place wings in a big bowl.

Step 2 - Combine all dry ingredients with the wings. (Smoked salt, pepper, grated garlic, grated ginger, chopped shallots, zest from orange and lemon, and finally the dill.) At this step I typically let the wings sit for a few hours in the fridge but you don't have to.

Step 3 - If you're letting the wings soak in the fridge for a few hours, now you can take them out. This is when I add the 2 cans of beer, lemon juice, orange juice, and pickle juice. Then I soak the wings anywhere from 24 to 36+ hours. The lemon and orange are acidic, so I wouldn't soak for more than 48 hours. All these ingredients really soak into the chicken and it's INCREDIBLE.

Step 4 - Choose your cooking method. I prefer to grill my wings but you can easily smoke them until an internal temperature of 165-175°F. I always shoot for a higher temperature of 175°F using an instant-read thermometer. At 175°F internal temperature, I feel the wings have a better mouth feel and are almost silky. You can also easily bake these wings until that internal temperature is where you want it. I would say bake at 375°F for 20 to 30 minutes.

Step 5 - ENJOY and eat wings! I eat and serve these wings plain, since the flavor is already so amazing. You can toss with your favorite buffalo or BBQ sauce before serving.

NOTE: Dill is my favorite herb other than basil. I buy one bunch of fresh dill and depending on how many wings you're making will depend on how much dill to use. I would take half for this recipe or about a handful. I don't chop the dill. I flip my chef's knife over to the dull side and I smack the dill to open it up and release the oils and fragrance, similar to using fresh lemongrass.

OUR QUARANTINE KITCHENS

SIDES

So many people tried each other's recipies.

From the Quarantine Kitchen of
Christine Zall

I have always loved to cook, I read cookbooks like some people read the newspaper–every day. I love to try different cuisines and enjoy recreating recipes for my family. I have a few unique challenges and that is my husband is allergic to dairy and cannot have milk, cheese, and creams. One son is a pescatarian and doesn't eat meat. So I am always trying to reinvent recipes to make it work for all of us.

My sons came home from college in March and were immediately on board in understanding that the grocery and food situation was going to be a challenge–we may not have everything at our fingertips. I have always kept a very well-stocked kitchen and pantry so that I can put together meals quickly, lots of frozen veggies, canned beans, rice, pasta etc.

You will see most of the ingredients here are things that can be a staple in a pantry. I had the shrimp frozen and was able to recreate this dish from a favorite restaurant of ours that was closed during the pandemic.

I am grateful we were healthy during all of this and that our extended family lived fairly close and I was able to cook and share meals with them, by leaving little packages on their doorsteps.

If we have learned anything through this it is the power and love that can be spread around the table and to be grateful that we have food on our table.

INGREDIENTS

2 tablespoons coconut oil (feel free to substitute butter or margarine)

2 eggs, scrambled

1 tablespoon vegetable or canola oil

1 ripe pineapple, chopped, scoop out and keep the outside to create a boat to present in

1 tablespoon sesame oil

12 oz. medium shrimp peeled and deveined, can substitute chicken or diced pork or leave out

4-6 garlic cloves minced

1 onion finely chopped

1 medium red bell pepper chopped

8 oz. frozen peas

1 tablespoon curry powder or more to taste

½ teaspoon ginger powder (or 1 ½ teaspoon fresh)

4 cups cooked, CHILLED long-grain rice like jasmine or basmati rice

1 cup raisins (I use yellow and regular)

½ cup unsalted roasted cashews

3 tablespoons fish sauce

½ tablespoon sugar

¼-½ teaspoon pepper

Salt to taste (I use ¼ teaspoon)

3 stalks green onions thinly sliced

PINEAPPLE FRIED RICE

The secret is to use cold rice, so if you have leftover rice this recipe is perfect. If not, just make rice, spread on a sheet pan, and put in the fridge for a half hour. The reason for this is warm rice has too much moisture and will end up sticking too much, absorbing liquids too quickly.

Heat coconut oil and vegetable oil in a hot pan, quickly scramble eggs and move to a separate bowl, then caramelize the chunks of pineapple that you cut out of the halved pineapple. Make sure they are fairly dry before adding to the pan by blotting with towels. Take out of the pan and put it in a separate bowl.

Add sesame oil to the pan. Then add shrimp into the pan and cook. Take out when cooked and add to bowl with pineapple. Chop both fine and leave to the side.

Then add in onion, bell pepper, and garlic. Sprinkle with ginger and curry powder, salt, and pepper; sauté till translucent.

Add in rice, making sure to incorporate with the onions, etc. Then press down in the pan. Let sit for a little, then turn and fold and press down so that the rice is getting fried, slowly putting in fish sauce and sugar that you mixed together. Turn a few times, then add in the raisins, cashews, and peas, and incorporate all. Then add back in the pineapple and shrimp and eggs.

Scoop into halved pineapples and sprinkle chopped scallions on top.

Remember this is your recipe and you know what your family likes. You can replace the shrimp with chicken or you can leave out completely. If you don't have peas you can add in finely chopped broccoli. If you don't have cashews use peanuts. You can substitute Craisins instead of raisins. It's a very forgiving recipe. I have added in chopped carrots. You can omit the eggs as well.

CAULIFLOWER FRITTERS

From the Quarantine Kitchen of
Diana Di Pilato

Boil cut up cauliflower until it's soft.

Beat eggs, salt, pepper, cheese, and parsley.

Mash the cauliflower and add it to the mix.

Add the bread crumbs a little at a time. You don't want it to be too dense. You may need more or less depending on the size of the cauliflower.

In a frying pan heat oil. Depending on how big your pan is, the oil should come up about ½ into the pan.

INGREDIENTS

One large cauliflower, cleaned and cut up

1 ½ cups grated cheese

Salt and pepper to taste

5 large eggs

1 cup of bread crumbs

¼ cup chopped parsley

Take one heaping table-spoon of the mix and fry until golden brown on each side.

From the Quarantine Kitchen of
Victoria Piccininni

INGREDIENTS

1 pound fresh mozzarella sliced into 3-4 long pieces

Flour

1 egg, beaten

Breadcrumbs

Vegetable oil

Sauce

Extra virgin olive oil

1 giant clove garlic grated or chopped

2 tomatoes diced (I used tomatoes on the vine)

1 cup white wine

Salt

Pepper

MOZZARELLA SPIEDINI

Cut fresh mozzarella into 3 to 4 slices, longways.

Dredge mozzarella in flour, then egg, then breadcrumb and fry.
Set aside to cool.

Sauce

Sauté 1 large garlic clove grated in extra virgin olive oil 30 seconds, add diced tomatoes, salt, and pepper. Let tomato cook down and mash it.

Add 1 cup of white wine and cook on medium for 5 minutes.

Plate the mozzarella and pour the sauce over. Serve immediately.

From the Quarantine Kitchen of
Christine Kanarick

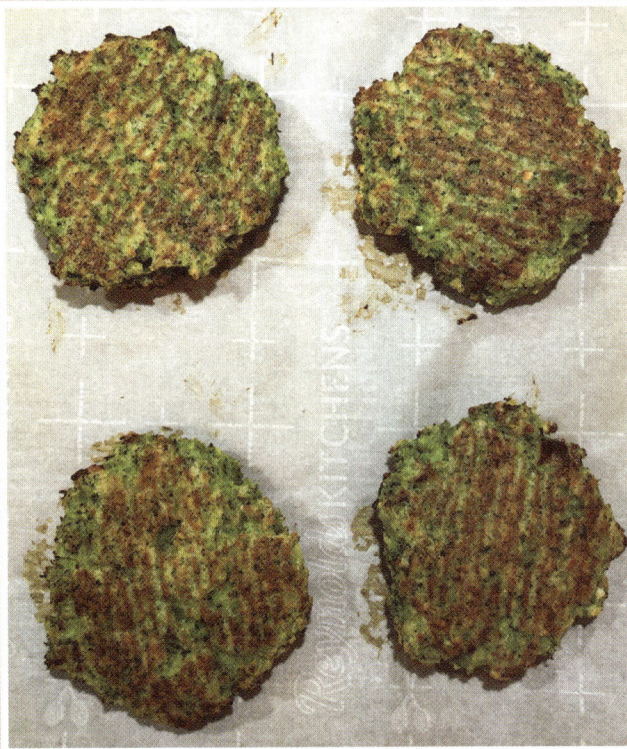

I am a baker. I absolutely love to bake and most of the things I make are high in calories. After baking almost daily for two months, I decided that it was time to get a little healthy. I found a recipe for baked broccoli cakes but it used fresh broccoli, which I didn't have. I decided to substitute frozen broccoli. It was a great way to use frozen vegetables that I stocked up on in quarantine. It is low in calories at 50 calories per cake, and I was still able to bake!

I have a 4-year-old daughter and a 6-year-old daughter. I loved cooking and baking in my previous life before I had children and when I had more free time. After having children, life got pretty busy and cooking and baking fell to the back burner. Since we have been quarantined, we have plenty of time to cook and bake together. My girls love learning how to make new recipes and I love spending so much time with them doing what I love, baking! Although being in quarantine is not always pleasant, I am grateful for the extra time I get to spend with my family everyday. We have baked a new recipe almost daily and besides family bonding time, I feel my girls are leaning math and science skills as well through cooking! The Quarantine Kitchen Facebook page has introduced us to new recipes and gives us something to look forward to trying each day. We're grateful for the community of people in Quarantine Kitchen and the administrators who put this all together.

Thank you!

INGREDIENTS

1 bag frozen broccoli (12 oz.)

1 egg

1 tablespoon garlic powder

1 teaspoon dried parsley

¼ cup scallions (green onions), chopped

½ cup parmesan cheese, grated

¼ cup flour

½ cup breadcrumbs (I used Panko)

½ teaspoon baking powder

2 teaspoon salt

1 teaspoon pepper

Cooking spray for pan

BROCCOLI CAKES

Preheat oven to 375°F.

Cook broccoli in microwave until defrosted (1 to 2 minutes) and then use a food processor to chop it finely.

In a large bowl, mix flour, baking powder, breadcrumbs, cheese, salt, and pepper.

Add shredded broccoli, garlic, parsley, and scallions to flour mixture. Toss to coat evenly.

Add egg and mix to combine well.

Line a sheet pan with parchment paper and spray with cooking spray.

Using a scoop, portion out broccoli cake mixture and use your hands to form broccoli cake. Press down to flatten.

Continue until broccoli cake mixture is gone, then bake for 20 to 25 minutes, flipping halfway through baking time.

NOTES
To fry the broccoli cakes: add enough oil to cover the bottom of a heavy skillet (like a cast iron pan). Scoop mixture and drop into hot oil. Use a spatula to slightly flatten broccoli cake. Cook for 5 minutes on each side. Drain on paper towel.

From the Quarantine Kitchen of
Alexa Panarella-Lopez

I created this recipe for one simple reason: to get my daughter and husband to eat more vegetables!

Let's be honest, cheese makes EVERYTHING better!

I grew up in an Italian-American household. My favorite memories revolve around food and family. I married my high school sweetheart! We share a love for many things but most importantly … for FOOD! When COVID-19 hit, my husband and I were forced to work remotely from home all while chasing around our toddler daughter. The world was filled with anxiety, but cooking and making our little family happy with these meals made me relaxed and feel a little at peace.

SPINACH BALLS

INGREDIENTS

2 packages of frozen chopped spinach

Shredded mozzarella

Grated cheese

Seasoned breadcrumbs

2 eggs

Pepper

Garlic powder

Defrost and drain spinach.

Combine with shredded mozzarella, seasoned breadcrumbs, and 2 eggs.

Add a sprinkle of grated cheese, garlic powder, and pepper.

Mix and roll into a ball.

Bake at 375°F for 30 minutes or until the spinach balls begin to turn golden/look crispy.

From the Quarantine Kitchen of
Karen Graine

"BREAD CAKES" also seen referred to as "Frogia, Froscias, Meudigas, or Breadballs," if shaped that way.

Whatever you call them, they're delicious and brought back a lot of memories for thousands of people on the Quarantine Kitchen page.

I learned that a lot of people put them in their sauce and some added mozzarella to the mixture.

So many knew of these and some didn't, but were curious to make them as well. It was so nice to see so many relate to something so simple.

Especially difficult times in isolation and pulling back to a simpler way of life—with many of us experiencing some sadness and uncertainty, the QK page and I believe, this "recipe" brought a smile to a lot of faces.

My grandmother made these, my great aunt, my mom and now I do. This is what is commonly learned in a lot of Italian homes, "nothing goes to waste!"

The leftover egg and breadcrumbs mixed together when finished breading and frying "cutlets" - usually chicken, veal, or pork.

INGREDIENTS

2 eggs

Salt & pepper

1 tablespoon grated cheese

1 cup seasoned breadcrumbs

BREAD CAKES

If made fresh:

Beat eggs and season with salt & pepper, grated cheese.

Mix together with breadcrumbs to form what looks like a dough, but not to runny.

Shape into oval "cakes."

Fry 1 to 2 minutes on medium heat on each side until brown.

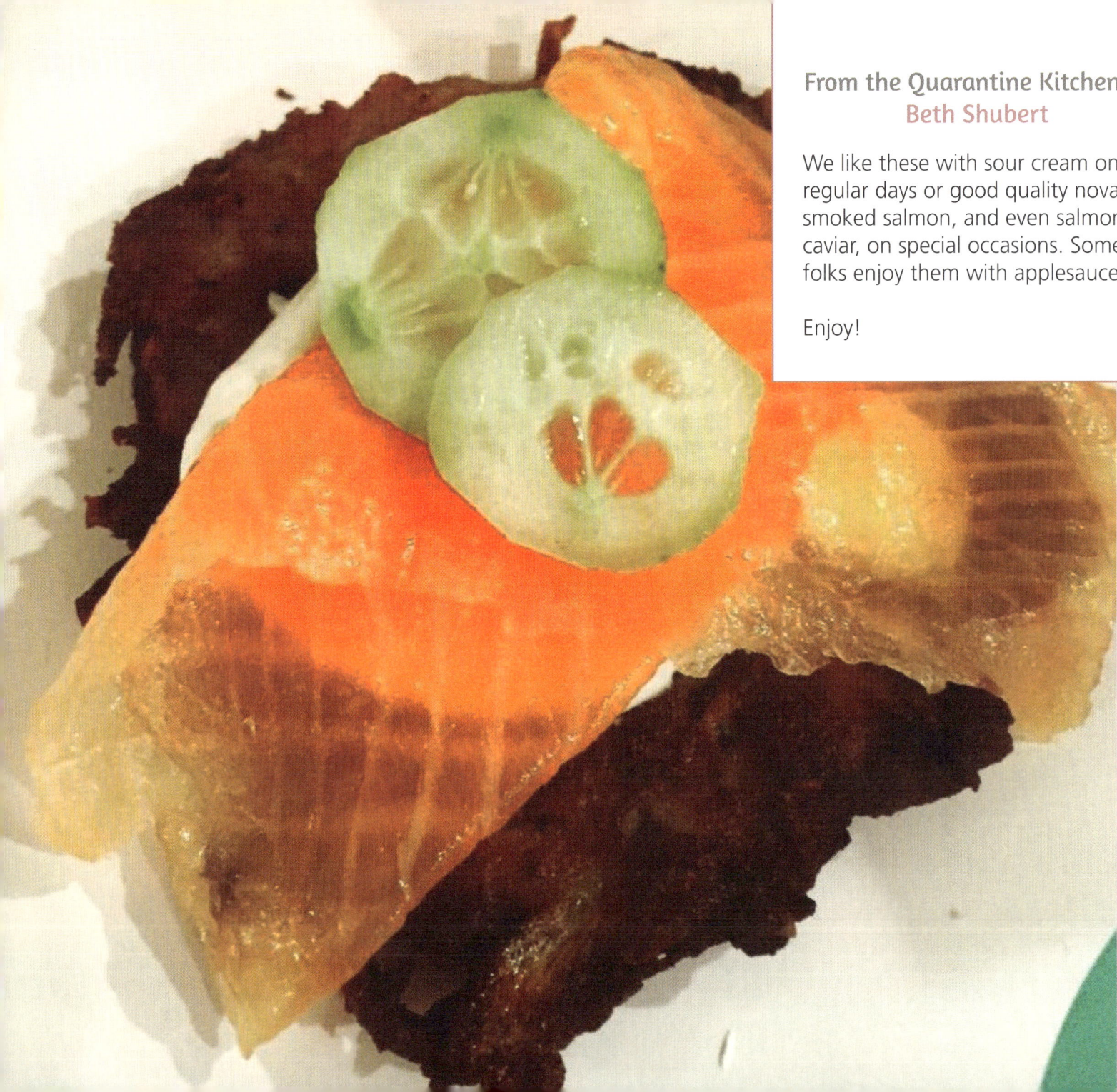

From the Quarantine Kitchen of
Beth Shubert

We like these with sour cream on regular days or good quality nova smoked salmon, and even salmon caviar, on special occasions. Some folks enjoy them with applesauce.

Enjoy!

POTATO PANCAKES

INGREDIENTS

4 large russet potatoes, peeled

1 very large onion

1 ½ teaspoons kosher or coarse salt

½ teaspoon black pepper

2 large eggs, beaten

3 tablespoons all-purpose flour

½ teaspoon baking soda

¾ cup minced fresh dill
(or 2 ½ teaspoons dried dill)

Canola and olive oil for frying

Grate potatoes and onion (I use a food processor).

Add to large bowl and then add the rest of the ingredients except the oil.

Heat ½ canola and ½ olive oil in heavy pan. The oil should be about ¼ deep in pan, and fairly hot but not smoking. You want the pancakes to crisp up but not burn. If pan is too cool, they will absorb too much oil before crisping; think of it as how you fry breaded chicken cutlets.

Drain the potato mixture (water will collect in bottom of bowl; potatoes may also start to discolor but it doesn't matter). I also squeeze each handful of the potato mixture between my palms or in a fist before placing in pan, so that the mixture is as dry as possible when it goes in the oil. I just find it fastest to use my hands.

Take handfuls (just under ½ cup of mixture for each pancake) of the potato mixture, squeeze in your hands to get any remaining water out, then flatten it a bit in your palms, and slide into pan. Be careful not to burn yourself. Use a large cooking spoon if you feel safer. Let cook about 2 to 3 minutes per side until deep brown. Flip each pancake. Cook an additional 2 to 3 minutes. Watch not to burn. After 3 batches or so you may need to add oils.

Have a plate with paper bag or a few layers of paper towel ready. As pancakes are done place them on the plate to let some of the oil drain off.

Taste one when cool and see if needs a sprinkling of salt. I usually do that as the pancakes come out.

From the Quarantine Kitchen of
Rosemarie Baldwin

Squash blossoms have been a delicacy in my family for as long as I can remember. On summer mornings, my grandpa would walk me out to the garden where we would cut the open squash blossoms that were not growing into zucchini fruit.

Later that evening, my mother would make this recipe. She inherited it from one of my grandmothers, although it's not clear which one. Both my maternal and paternal grandmothers were Italian—one from Sicily and the other from Naples. This picture is of me as a baby with both of them.

As with many Italian recipes, they are passed on through oral traditions. Most of the time, family members do not have recipes written down—and do not use exact measurements. It is a right of passage to be able to perfect a recipe passed down orally based on just instinct (and practice).

During quarantine 2020, I spent a lot of time cooking and baking with my children, and teaching them our Italian recipes. I also started to write down some recipes so that my children would always have them, and would know from where they originated in our family.

So, I hope you enjoy making our family's zucchini squash blossom recipe. They taste like summer and beloved family traditions.

ZUCCHINI SQUASH BLOSSOMS

INGREDIENTS

8-10 squash blossoms

2 eggs

A little milk to loosen eggs

1 teaspoon baking soda

2 tablespoons flour

Salt/pepper/garlic powder to taste

Recipe *(based on my grandmother's oral recipe)*

Wash and chop blossoms into quarters. Set aside.

Mix all ingredients with whisk, then add chopped blossoms.

Heat oil (I use canola) in a cast iron skillet.

Drop mixture by heaping spoonful into hot oil.

Turn when brown.

Drain on paper towel.

Enjoy!

INGREDIENTS

2 cups uncooked long grain rice

Salt and pepper to taste

1 tablespoon olive oil

1 pound ground sirloin

¼ cup onion, chopped

5 oz. frozen peas

2 cups homemade tomato sauce

1 large egg, 1 egg white

½ cup Pecorino Romano cheese, or parmesan

Cooking spray

4 tablespoons seasoned Italian breadcrumbs, divided

1 ¼ cup shredded mozzarella

RICE BALL CASSEROLE

Cook rice with salt to taste according to package directions. Set aside to cool.

Meanwhile, sauté ground sirloin in olive oil; cook until brown. Add onions and sauté a few more minutes until they are soft.

Season with salt and pepper and add peas and 1 cup sauce; simmer on low, covered, about 20 minutes.

Preheat oven to 400°F.

In a large bowl combine cooked rice, Pecorino Romano, eggs, and ½ cup tomato sauce and mix well.

Spray a 9 x 13 casserole dish with cooking spray, making sure to spray sides too. Add 2 tablespoons breadcrumbs to the dish and roll around to coat the bottom and sides.

Take half of the rice mixture and spread evenly. Top with all the meat and peas mixture.

Top with ¾ cup mozzarella cheese.

Cover with remaining rice and spread evenly. Top with remaining sauce, remaining 2 tablespoons breadcrumbs, and remaining ½ cup mozzarella.

Cover with foil and bake 30 minutes. Uncover and cook for another 5 to 10 minutes until it browns a little on top.

OUR QUARANTINE KITCHENS

PASTA

Many original pasta dishes were shared by so many!

Although I am of Sicilian descent, I have always loved to try different regional dishes of Italy. Italy is a culinary experience and each region has its own beauty and authenticity. And as a Sicilian living in America, I wanted to create the same beauty and authenticity from the comfort of my own home. I tried many renditions of the Barese dish, Orecchiette con Cime di Rapa e Salsiccia, but I wanted to recreate it my way. I wanted to remain true to this classic recipe, while still incorporating my Sicilian roots. From using extra virgin olive oil from my trees in Sicily, to bringing on the heat of crushed pepper, as almost every Sicilian does, this dish was the perfect mix of two regions coming together.

I am a first-generation Sicilian-American and grew up with the most amazing cooks surrounding me. My cooking journey began at the very age of three when my Nonna taught me how to "beat 2 eggs" to make the perfect scrambled eggs. And from that age on, I was intrigued by anything and everything that had to do with food. I looked at food as both a science and a skill that one had to master. In my eyes, my two idols, my dear mother and Nonna Madeline, have both mastered this skill. They attribute to my culinary success.

Over the years, cooking has become my form of therapy. An outlet for me to explore different dishes, cultures, and flavors. Every dish that I make, one way or another, is a story of my past, my culture, and my experiences in life. That is the beauty of cooking; creating a masterpiece to be admired and enjoyed by all. One day, I hope to retell my story with pages filled with savory art that pay homage to my family, my culture, and my future.

INGREDIENTS

1 pound of orecchiette pasta

2 pounds of broccoli rabe

1 pound of sausage meat with fennel

1 cup of chicken stock

4 tablespoons of extra virgin olive oil

5-6 cloves of garlic

½ teaspoon of crushed red pepper

1 tablespoon of salt

Pinch of crushed black pepper

1 ½ tablespoons of grated Parmigiano-Reggiano Cheese

ORECCHIETTE AND SPINACH

In a large skillet, sauté the garlic with extra virgin olive oil for about five minutes. Next, add the sausage and lightly brown it.

Add the chicken stock to the skillet along with crushed red pepper, crushed black pepper, salt, and grated cheese; stir on simmer.

Prepare and clean your broccoli rabe as a pot of water is boiling.

Add the broccoli rabe to boiling water and cook it for about five minutes.

Next, drain your broccoli rabe, chop it into smaller pieces, and add it to the skillet with the sausage mixture.

Finally, boil the orecchiette pasta for 10 minutes; drain the pasta and combine it into the skillet with all the other ingredients and mix well.

Buon Appetito!

The kitchen was the center of our household when I was growing up. My family was and still is always in the kitchen! I was one of those quiet observers when I was a kid, just there watching my family and enjoying the bustle while they prepared meals whether it be for the usual family dinner or larger occasions. We always hosted large family events, and food has always brought us together. There was a never a time when we would make a small meal, not even if it was just the immediate family. We cook big! While growing up, I spent so much time soaking it all in, learning the recipes and techniques, and then later preparing these feasts myself in my own kitchen. The kitchen is a place of comfort and solace for me. Cooking and baking both help me to relax, even more so now during this pandemic. It has been even more comforting being part of a community that shares this passion. The camaraderie of Quarantine Kitchen is so calming and brings me joy. It is also especially rewarding to be able to share my favorite meals and recipes with others during this rough time. I hope for everyone to feel the same comfort I do when cooking these meals. To be able to reach out and share with so many people all around the world is amazing. Just as it always has for my family, food is bringing us all together. Bringing us all together during a time when we need each other most. I am so glad to be a part of it.

INGREDIENTS

1 pound anelletti pasta (ringed shaped), cooked al' dente at least 3 minutes before cooking time on package, cooled down and set aside

1 pound chopped meat, cooked until you see no pink; drain the fat out

Homemade red sauce

Homemade sautéed peas

¼ cup freshly grated parmesan

Salt and pepper to taste

16 oz. mozzarella shredded

For sautéed peas:

1 pound bag of frozen baby peas
Extra virgin olive oil
2 large white onions
Onion powder
Salt and pepper

Homemade sauce:

(2) 16 oz. cans peeled crushed tomatoes
Extra virgin olive oil
1 head of garlic
Italian seasoning
Salt and pepper
1 teaspoon of sugar

BAKED RING PASTA

Pea recipe

Cut and dice onions. In a medium pot, put a layer of olive oil, enough to coat onions. Preheat oil then add chopped onions. Brown onions until golden.

Add frozen peas and stir together with onions. Cover peas and onions with water.

Add 2 tablespoons of onion powder to pea mixture. Salt and pepper to taste. Let peas cook. When water starts to boil, lower flame. Let simmer for 2 hours, stirring occasionally until water starts to evaporate. Taste frequently and add spices to your taste.

Sauce recipe

Start by peeling garlic. After peeled, I crush it and cut it up.

In sauce pan, put a light layer of olive oil enough to fry garlic. Keep a eye on garlic and brown; stir frequently or it will stick.

Have your crushed tomatoes ready. When garlic is slightly browned, add crushed tomatoes.

Add Italian seasoning and salt and pepper to taste.

Cook on low flame. When the sauce starts to simmer, add sugar and let cook for about an hour.

Once the sauce, peas, and chopped meat are done; in the pot with the cooked pasta, start adding sauce, chopped meat, peas, mozzarella, and grated cheese. Add a little at a time until your desired consistency (adding more, extra meat, extra peas, etc.). Once combined, add a little mozzarella to the top of pasta and bake in a preheated oven of 350°F for 30 minutes.

From the Quarantine Kitchen of
Lisa Mercante

A friend of mine invited me to the Quarantine Kitchen Facebook group and I have to say, it has been a true blessing to me as it has given me something to look forward to each and everyday. I love reading the recipes, seeing photos of other members' creations, and, of course, seeing the beautiful kitchens where all of the recipes and cooking memories are made. Prior to the quarantine, I cooked, but definitely not as much as I am cooking now. As a full-time working mother of two teenage boys and my very many events and practices and deadlines to meet, my time was limited and I was being pulled in 100 different directions and I never had the time to cook like I would have liked. Thankfully, I've been blessed with a husband who cooks a lot. I now find that I have the time and I have embraced this experience to try to create different dishes that maybe I would not have ordinarily made. I also find myself baking much more. I have found some really wonderful recipes on the site and I look forward to continuing to utilize these recipes when the quarantine is over. I've made spaghetti Bolognese, a light vodka sauce, eggplant rollatini, banana bread, fresh chocolate chip cookies, chocolate covered matzoh; dishes and treats that I have never made and/or have not made in the recent past. I truly love the warmth and positivity I have found on this site as well as some of the new friends I have made!

INGREDIENTS

¾ pound of pasta (I used penne rigate but you can use whatever pasta you like)

¾ cup of extra virgin olive oil

½ stick of butter

2 sliced garlic cloves

½ cup of parmesan cheese

¾ cup of breadcrumbs
(I use 4C breadcrumbs)

¾ cup of Panko breadcrumbs

¾ cup of heavy cream
(plus more if you need)

Pinch of pink sea salt plus more to taste (or whatever salt you have)

You can add pepper to taste, but I do not like pepper.

BUTTER BREADCRUMBS PASTA

Boil water, add a pinch of salt to the water. Boil your pasta until al dente (it will cook a bit more at the end).

Remove pasta from the pot when done and set aside.

Use the same pot you used for the pasta and add ¼ stick of butter and ¼ cup of olive oil to the pot on a low to medium flame, add garlic and brown your garlic. (About 1 to 2 minutes).

Add both cups of breadcrumbs to the garlic, butter, and oil, add another ¼ cup of olive oil and brown the breadcrumbs. (Be sure to continuously stir).

Add pinch of salt and the ½ cup of parmesan cheese to the bread-crumb mixture as you continue to stir.

Add the already cooked pasta to the pot and mix all together (with a spoon) so that the pasta is covered with the breadcrumb mixture. (1 to 2 minutes).

Add the heavy cream to the pasta and breadcrumb mixture along with the remaining ¼ cup of olive oil and mix (about a minute).

Let sit for 2 minutes and serve!

Enjoy!

Spices oh Spices, what do I use you for? Members say:

Rosemary with lamb, thyme or sage with mushrooms, turkey; tarragon with chicken; basil with anything Italian and especially tomatoes; oregano with anything Greek.

I use salt, pepper and garlic on everything. If I want a distinct flavor or certain foods, I add other spices. For example, I use sage on lamb and turkey.

I love using turmeric. I sprinkle a good shake on my chicken breast with garlic and onion powders, paprika, and salt and pepper with oil as my standard grill blend. My kids love it.

For myself in my culture of cooking (Peruvian), we always start with a base of what we call a sofrito-which just means to sauté ingredients ... we use onion, garlic, tomato, and peppers, diced finely and sautéed in a pan. We add salt, pepper, and paprika if making a red base, like for stews. For marinating pork or chicken we might use cumin, paprika salt, peper, garlic, and red/white vinegar and let sit over night.

I use lemon pepper on roasted veggies. Ginger, I love on fish. Rosemary and thyme I use with any chicken. I like turmeric on veggies, too!

To me, using spices is like painting. Is a matter of creativity and taste. Then you progress like in sciences development, by trial and error.

Mexican food is going to be pepper and cumin and garlic and onion; Southern Cajun is cayenne pepper, paprika, a tiny bit of oregano, white pepper, black pepper, garlic, onion powder, and dry mustard if you can find it. If you're making something with turkey and chicken and want kind of a Thanksgiving flavor, you can use sage, rosemary, and thyme.

Fresh grated nutmeg for cream sauces.

I made a homemade rub with black pepper, garlic powder, onion powder and cinnamon ... yes, cinnamon. I would never think about cinnamon on beef ribs but it was awesome.

Try 'em all out. If it doesn't taste good, you move on. Trial & error!

FARFALLE

My recipe for Farfalle is my Mom's (Marie), with no written recipe, although I begged her for years to write things down.

She used to say, "We're Italian, you smell, taste, and eat." She passed away in 2001 of cancer.

Boil the Farfalle. Sauté garbanzo beans, red kidney beans, and white kidney beans. When done, add together with parmesan and olive oil infused with garlic and basil.

I'm a retired NYC Detective, I worked 31 years, mostly in Manhattan.

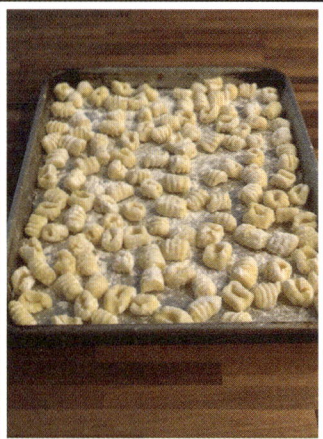

From the Quarantine Kitchen of
Raffaella Pernice

Growing up in Italy, meals were very important and well planned:

Domenica (Sunday) sauce, and a roast (never had sauce with meatballs for Sunday dinner).

Lunedì (Monday) left over.

Martedì (Tuesday) soups.

Mercoledì (Wednesday) vary, usually a dish with plenty of vegetables.

Giovedì (Thursday) GNOCCHI.

Venerdì (Friday) pizza or fish.

Sabato (Saturday) anything goes.

Gnocchi di Patate, the fluffiest pasta you will ever have.

INGREDIENTS

4 medium Idaho potatoes (basically one per person)

1 ½ cups of flour

1 egg

A pinch of salt

GIOVEDÌ GNOCCHI

Place the potatoes with the skin in pot with cold water, and bring it to a boil.

Boil for about 30 to 40 minutes, until you can easily go through potatoes with the knife.

Drain and peel the potatoes when they are still warm, place them in a potato ricer.

Mix the potatoes with the egg and salt.

Roll the dough in long round shape (snake like). The size may vary for your preference.

Cut in ¼ inch pieces. You can cook them like this, or if you want them a little prettier, roll the dough gently with two fingers over a fork. This may be tricky but the gnocchi with the grooves will hold the sauce so much better.

Important: when you boil gnocchi, as soon as they start to float, drain them, they are ready (a couple of minutes).

Buon Appetito!

From the Quarantine Kitchen of
Leah Fernandez

My grandma Antoinette made the best, and I mean the best, Sunday sauce in all of Brooklyn! Growing up, a lot of my time was spent in the kitchen watching her cook; these are some of my greatest memories. When my grandmother was diagnosed with Alzheimer's disease, I took over a lot of the cooking, including the holidays and Sunday dinners. This recipe, which is loved by many, is an ode to my grandma, but with a twist! I hope you enjoy it as much as my family does.

GRANDMA'S SUNDAY SAUCE WITH A TWIST

INGREDIENTS

1 ½ tablespoons olive oil

1 tablespoon sundried tomato paste

1-2 tablespoons of sugar, depending on level of sweetness that you prefer

1 small onion, finely chopped

2 cloves of garlic, finely chopped

(1) 28 oz. can of crushed tomatoes, with or without basil

(1) 6 oz. can of tomato paste

Salt and pepper, to taste

In a large sauce pan, heat olive oil over medium heat. Add onion and garlic, sauteing until soft; about 2 minutes. Add sundried tomato paste and sugar to the pan, stirring to combine. Cook for another 2 to 3 minutes, until onions and garlic look slightly caramelized.

Turn heat to low and add both the crushed tomatoes and tomato paste. Stir until tomato paste is well incorporated. Season with salt and pepper.

Cover and cook on low for 3 hours, stirring frequently.*

Once finished, serve over your favorite pasta or incorporate into your favorite dishes.

* If you notice that the sauce is too thick, you may add water, ¼ cup at a time.

From the Quarantine Kitchen of
Elizabeth Zollo

I've been married 4 years and I am a mother to an 11 month old. I've never been much of a cook. Every so often I would find a recipe I would be interested in trying and that was the extent of my cooking experience. However, I love to eat and try new things. I married into a family of cooks; my husband has owned a restaurant and now a pizzeria since we've been together. I was always very intimidated to cook for him and his family. Since quarantine began for me back in March, I started to cook dinner every night; let's face it, there isn't much else to do. Over the past few months I began to get more comfortable in the kitchen and have grown to actually enjoy cooking. After rotating the same recipes, you get bored fast. That's when my husband told me about Quarantine Kitchen and I joined in the hope of finding some new recipes to try out. I'm actually addicted to going on the page now, people have come up with such creative recipes, and every time I'm on there I get hungry looking at all the delicious pictures. I especially enjoy being on the page because everyone respects the guidelines of being part of the group; everyone is positive and helpful, there are no debates or politics which it seems are everywhere you turn now. I very much enjoy scrolling through the page each night after I put my son to bed. That's why I was very excited to hear that a cookbook was going to be created from all the great recipes. My recipe is not one that was passed down from generations that has a sentimental story; it was just something I came up with that I wanted to give a shot. I took my knowledge from some recipes that my husband has taught me, and from what I've been learning through the Facebook page and combined it to come up with a pretty enjoyable dish. I want to share it in hopes that many other families can enjoy it as well!

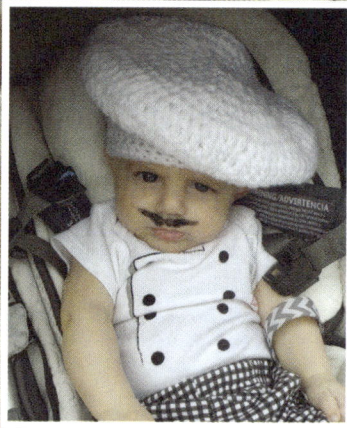

INGREDIENTS

Pasta:

1 pound paccheri pasta

2 pound container of ricotta

¼ pound thin sliced prosciutto

Sauce:

1 tablespoon extra virgin olive oil

1 teaspoon minced garlic

8 oz. container of pre sliced mushrooms

A few slices of prosciutto, diced

1 oz. sherry wine

1 teaspoon salt

½ teaspoon pepper

1 teaspoon parsley

Dash of Gravy Master

1 cup chicken broth

¾ stick of butter

Flour as needed

STUFFED PASTA IN SHERRY WINE BUTTER SAUCE

Boil pasta in salted water. Drain when pasta is al dente and run under cold water to cool off.

In a pastry bag combine ricotta and diced prosciutto. Fill each individual pasta and place it upright in a large oven-safe baking pan. Continue this with the entire pound until all pasta is stuffed. When the tray is full pour a little bit of chicken broth just to cover the bottom of the pan. Place in oven on 350°F for ½ hour or until the top of the pasta is slightly brown.

While pasta is in the oven, begin your sauce. In a non-stick large pan, heat oil and garlic, until garlic is slightly brown. Then, add in mushrooms, salt, and pepper, and sauté on a medium-high flame for about 5 minutes. Add diced prosciutto and move ingredients around in the pan for 1 minute. Turn flame up and add in sherry wine and let cook for 1 minute. Turn down flame to medium and add in chicken broth, parsley, and Gravy Master and let simmer for 20 minutes. Put the flame on medium/low and add in butter, stirring slowly. The sauce should begin to thicken, so then add in flour. Let simmer for another 30 seconds, shut flame, and let set before serving. (If you prefer a brothy sauce, add chicken broth. If you prefer a thicker sauce add more butter and a drop more flour.)

When pasta is ready, scoop into the dish and pour the sauce over the pasta. Add a sprinkle of grated Pecorino Romano cheese and it's ready to serve. Buon Appetito!

I love the Quarantine Kitchen cooking Page. It has offered me so much information I didn't know about cooking and baking, as well as new recipes. The people are so nice, too.

Thanks.

This is a recipe I made up as I went along, but it turned out so good.

Very basic, very simple.

KAT'S EASY HEALTHY PASTA

INGREDIENTS

Spaghetti No. 8

Spinach (fresh, frozen, or canned)

Asparagus

Garlic

Ricotta cheese

Grated parmesan cheese

Salt

Pepper

Olive oil

Boil water and cook pasta.

Sautè the spinach with garlic (as much or as little as you like).

Grill the asparagus (I do mine in my air fryer or oven).

Add all ingredients in with the pasta.

Top with scoops of ricotta cheese. Mix.

Add salt and pepper and grated cheese.

SPINACH AND MUSHROOM STUFFED SHELLS

From the Quarantine Kitchen of
Kristen Allain

Prep:
Thaw the spinach in the microwave and use paper towels or a clean kitchen towel to wring out all the liquid.

Remove the stems from the mushrooms and slice them to roughly the same thickness. Don't worry about neatness, this is to ensure even cooking of everything.

To cook:
Preheat the oven to 350°F.

Cook the shells a minute short of package directions. They will finish cooking in the oven once stuffed.

Melt butter in a sautè pan. Add the sliced mushrooms, garlic, shallots, and cook until you can smell the fragrant mushrooms. Once the mushrooms are cooked, pour the contents of the pan into a food processor and pulse to mince the mixture. Pour this into a mixing bowl, and add the spinach, cheeses, and a pinch of nutmeg. Stir to mix the stuffing.

Ladle some sauce in your baking dish. You don't need a lot, just enough to cover the bottom of the pan so the shells don't stick to it.

Fill each shell with the stuffing, a tablespoon is a good tool for this.

Line the baking dish with the shells, I usually offset the rows to squeeze more in.

Drizzle more sauce on top of the shells, and bake at 350°F for 20 minutes. Remove pan from oven, top with more mozzarella cheese, and bake for another 15 minutes or until the cheese melts.

INGREDIENTS

10 oz. frozen chopped spinach

1 pound cremini mushrooms

2 cloves garlic, cracked

1 shallot, sliced

16 oz. ricotta cheese

1 cup shredded mozzarella cheese (for stuffing)

Pinch nutmeg

Salt/pepper to taste

1 pound jumbo shells

Marinara sauce of your choosing; I like homemade, but jarred works in a pinch

From the Quarantine Kitchen of
Graig Martin, Esq.

INGREDIENTS

1 cup vodka (any)

1 ½ teaspoon crushed red pepper

4 tablespoons olive oil

4 cloves of garlic, minced

1 tablespoon of fresh parsley

1 tablespoon of dried parsley

1 tablespoon dried basil

1 tablespoon fresh basil

Prosciutto, chopped (¼ thick diced imported preferred)

(2) 28 oz. cans crushed tomatoes

(4) 8 oz. cans tomato sauce

16 oz. of water

2 cups of heavy cream

Salt and pepper

Pecorino Romano to taste

GRAIG'S SECRET VODKA SAUCE

Soak the red pepper in the vodka for 30 minutes.

Sauté the prosciutto, garlic, parsley, basil, salt, and pepper until it browns.

Pour in vodka. Simmer for 10 minutes.

Stir in crushed tomatoes, tomato sauce, and 16 oz. of water. Simmer 10 minutes.

Stir in heavy cream and parmesan.

Boil water for pasta.

Pour vodka sauce over pasta once strained and in bowl.

From the Quarantine Kitchen of
Patricia Viscardi

Cooking was always part of my Mom's household. She learned from her mother and taught all of her four children. How lucky we were …

I remember all the traditional dishes, Wednesday and Sunday, always a pasta dish! All the special holiday Italian pies. How lucky we were …

Every year, before Christmas I recall my father driving me to my Aunt Dolly's house and together with my Aunt, I would bake 10 to15 types of cookies … how lucky was I … from that, and years later, I considered myself a baker and cook, not a professional but nonetheless.

INGREDIENTS

Pancake

4 eggs

2 cups of flour

⅔ cups of cold water

1 stick of butter

Tomato Sauce

Italian tomato & basil sauce is preferable

3 pound container of ricotta cheese

1 large roll of mozzarella cheese, chopped up in small pieces

1 egg

Parsley

MOM'S HOMEMADE MANICOTTI

Pancake
Combine all ingredients together and make sure the batter is very watery (might need to add in additional water if necessary).
This process is to make sure the pancake is very thin.

Pour a large spoon of batter into a slightly oiled frying pan - spread to cover the pan, making sure the pancake is evenly spread around the pan. Cook each side a few minutes.

This recipe makes approximately 20 to 25 pancake crepes. Layer each with parchment paper so they don't stick together.

Pancake Stuffing
Combine all tomato sauce ingredients together and set aside.

Place the pancake flat and scoop in a good handful of ricotta stuffing into center of pancake and roll it closed. Place in an oiled baking pan, layering them side by side.

Once they are all rolled and stuffed in pan, start pouring the tomato sauce on top. Sprinkle some grated cheese on top or put mozzarella slices on top (optional).

Bake for 350°F for 1 hour, or until nice and crispy.

ZAK'S PEANUT BUTTER COOKIES

INGREDIENTS

2 ½ cups all-purpose flour

1 teaspoon baking soda

½ teaspoon baking powder

½ teaspoon kosher salt

1 cup (2 sticks) butter, softened

1 cup granulated sugar

1 cup packed brown sugar

2 large eggs

¼ teaspoon vanilla

1 ½ cups creamy peanut butter
(if 16.3 oz., use the whole jar)

DIRECTIONS

In a large bowl, whisk together flour, baking soda, baking powder, and salt.

Using stand or hand mixer, beat butter and sugars on medium speed until very fluffy, 2 minutes. Beat in eggs one at a time, mixing well after each addition. Add peanut butter and continue mixing until mixture is completely smooth and fluffy, 2 to 3 minutes more.

Add flour mixture in batches and continue mixing, scraping sides of bowl as you go. Refrigerate batter 1 hour.

When ready to bake, preheat oven to 350°F. Drop tablespoons of dough on prepared baking sheets, about 2 inches apart. (I use a small ice cream scoop and roll into a ball then place them on a cookie sheet.)

Using a fork, score cookies with a cross-hatch pattern.

Bake until golden, 15 to 18 minutes. Transfer to wire rack to let cool before serving.

The Quarantine Kitchen family was blessed to have the life of a man and his dog add a layer of love to our days. Zak was a rockstar, and Mike quickly gained thousands of followers who looked forward to the evening post and the London broil Zak so enjoyed. As Zak's health started to take a turn (my eyes well-up thinking about this), the members showed a daily outpouring of love, support and genuine concern to Mike and Zak. When it came time for Zak to leave us, the members were beside themselves. They just couldn't say enough or do enough to support our extended family, Mike and Zak. I believe it was meant to be that we all were there for Mike and Zak, and Zak will not only hold a place in each of our hearts, but now his amazing life is forever documented in our cookbook. For this I say divine intervention somehow always plays a role.

~ Traci Cangiano

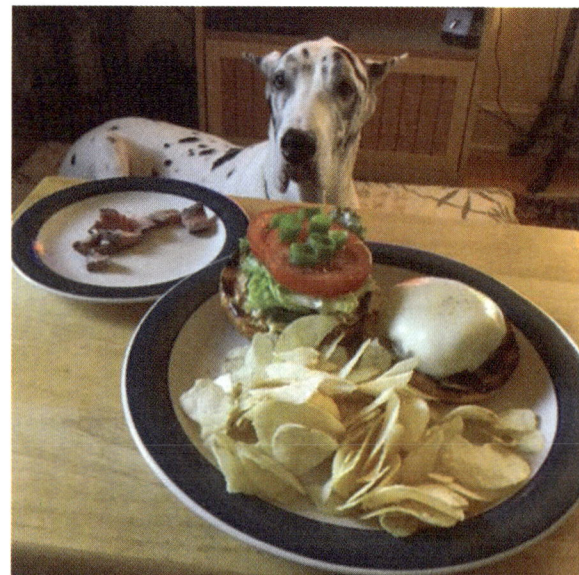

From the Quarantine Kitchen of
Mike Hill

Zak is a dog. Mike Hill is his human.

Hi everyone my name is Zak and I want to thank you for allowing me to be part of this wonderful group and in your cookbook!

I'm an 11-year-old Harlequin Great Dane. I rescued my human Mike Hill ten years ago and he became my family.

I was abused, thin, and didn't trust people back then and would become very aggressive when he tried to get me out of my crate! That didn't last long once I got to know him.

I've slowed down a bit now that I have arthritis in my back legs and bone cancer of my right shoulder. My right leg just hangs there now and I can't put any weight on it. My back hips have trouble holding me up, but Mike goes behind me when I get up to go out in case my back legs give out, and sometimes they do, so he catches me on the way down! He's got my back.

I used to go to physical therapy every other week and get acupuncture, massages, and shots of Adequan, but I can't anymore! I'm just not mobile enough now. I really miss it, too! I loved all the attention! Now, Mike gives me Galliprant which is an anti-inflammatory and Dasuquin for my joints. It helps me but sometimes it upsets my stomach and I lose my appetite!

Mike does what he can to make me eat, so I work him for London Broil and/or chicken breast or thighs! So are you ready for this? Lately I've been refusing to eat out of my bowl or off of my snack plate Mike makes me, so we can eat together, now I'm making him hand feed me! Can you believe that? He even puts my dry dog food on my bed to make me eat, then keeps putting it in a pile in front of me so I don't have any trouble reaching it! Now that he's joined this group, I get extra food and my picture taken every night! He's not that great of a cook, but it's better than the sandwiches he used to eat before! I think he's a lot more motivated and inspired since he started with the Quarantine Kitchen website and I'm eating better now too!

He tells me I'm quite popular and people are behind me all the way to keep going and fighting this cancer thing! They are sending their love, prayers, good vibes, good energy, you name it, just for me and Mike!

Here's to hoping I will be around for a few more years and thank you all for being so kind, supportive, encouraging and most of all, loving!

~ Zak

"... Everyone's been telling me I'll know and he'll tell you when it's time and that's exactly what's happening! I know without a doubt it's time! Zak will be crossing over tomorrow morning at around 11 a.m. at home in my arms and me telling him how much I love him and what he means to me!

... He's resting comfortably, no crying, no cheek puffing when he breathes, and no signs of pain unless he tries to get up and move. I gave him extra meds so I think that's helping! He's eating ice cubes, but now refuses everything else, even my peanut butter cookies!

... My head is spinning with the thoughts of so many memories and the overwhelming response to end of Zak's journey from QK!
The picture on the right was Zak last night. The bottom is Zak this morning.

... Zak went out in his royal attitude, with class and dignity! It was very peaceful! The Lap Of Love vet was more than patient, understanding and compassionate! He was also very taken back by Zak's overwhelming popularity and support from this family! He was literally overwhelmed!

... He also, from his evaluation, agreed with me that Zak had fluids in his lungs and the cancer traveled into them as well as his spine, but was amazed that Zak wasn't in any signs of pain but was in breathing distress. Which means he wasn't receiving enough oxygen in his lungs and very shortly organs will be shutting down. He agreed it was time before the pain started. That made things a lot easier about making this decision!

... Thank you everyone, I have so much more to say, but just at the moment I just don't have it in me now! I hope this post helps make it a little bit easier, lift up your spirits and sadness!"

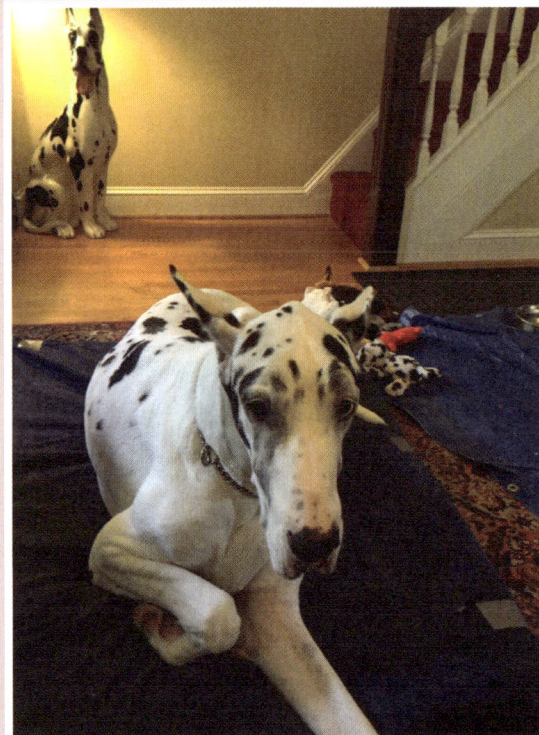

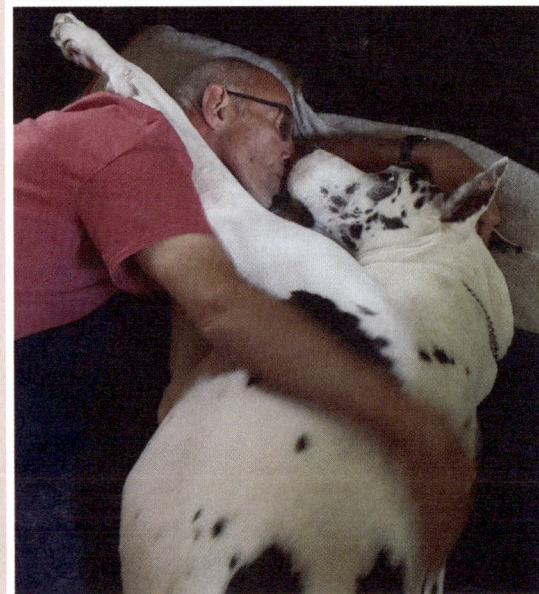

A sample of support from Quarantine Kitchen members posted on the Quarantine Kitchen page:

... Mike I know you feel the love.. you have 1000's of people that shed tears for Zak and you. Thank you for sharing your best friend with all of us. I do hope that you come back to us soon. We all need friends like you. RIP you beautiful angel pup. We will miss that face..

... So much love and support to you and Zak ❤️ he couldn't have had a better partner throughout his life. Time heals but the memories never leave, thank you for letting us take part in yours and Zak's journey. Sending prayers and well wishes your way 😔 ❤️

... My heart is broken for beautiful Zak, but also for you Mike. You were the best dad ever. You both were blessed to have each other 💌 🙏 Sending you love, hugs and prayers. I so enjoyed your post every night ❤️ Thank you for all the smiles

... His life was beautiful because of you and yours because of him. I hope the wonderful memories and love get you through this very difficult time. I am so very sorry for the loss of your beautiful Zak 💙🐾. Rest easy sweet boy. ((💙🐾))

... I'm so so sorry for your loss Mike! I can only imagine your sadness after spending 11 wonderful years. I've just been following for about a month and am wiping tears as I write this. God bless you for the wonderful care you gave your boy! Prayers, blessings and love to you during this time!

It's the most unselfish thing you could ever do for him Mike 💜 he will always be an angel looking over you, romping and cloud hopping, eating every peanut butter cookie in sight. He will be free of any pain or illness and when the time comes, he'll be at the Rainbow Bridge waiting patiently for you 💜 🌈🐶🌈 We will miss him and hope you stay connected – there are thousands here for you, you are not alone and many of us have experienced the same pain😢 Give Zak a million kisses from all of us. To say he is loved is putting it lightly 💜

OUR QUARANTINE KITCHENS

MAIN COURSES

Everyone loved watching what each other cooked for dinner,
and you can bet that many familes across
the U.S. and beyond may have just
shared the very same meals.

If I could come up with two positives from the "coronavirus-safe-at-home-quarantine," it would be, most importantly, spending more quality time with my family and being able to make more elaborate family dinners to share with the ones I love. I've been enjoying the process of sharing the recipes I make for my family on my blog and several social media forums like the Quarantine Kitchen.

The background behind this savory chicken dish was a traditional shrimp scampi recipe that my mother taught me a few months before she passed away. I never had an interest in learning the recipe from her when I was younger because I personally don't like seafood. As my husband and sons began asking me to make some seafood dishes at home, I turned to her and asked her for guidance. Scampi was something she had always made throughout my childhood (It was also known as hotdog night for Rachel!), so she was the resident expert. Nine years later, I still use her base sauce for this chicken dish but you could definitely use it for any type of white fish, shrimp, or scallops.

HOMEMADE LEMON GARLIC CHICKEN

INGREDIENTS

3 boneless, skinless chicken breasts cleaned and cut into strips

Salt & pepper, to taste

4 cloves fresh minced garlic

4 tablespoons butter

4 tablespoons olive oil

¾ cup dry white wine

¾ cup chicken broth

2 lemon wedges

Fresh shaved parmesan

Chopped parsley for garnish

Lemon wedges for garnish

1 pound angel hair pasta or spaghetti, cooked, to serve over

For this recipe I always use a cast iron skillet, it gives the chicken a very nice sear. While I recommended it, you don't necessarily have to use cast iron, but it gets the best results.

Salt and pepper the chicken, sear it in the butter and olive oil until it's golden brown.

Lower your cooking heat to medium-low and add your fresh minced garlic. Be fast with this step as you don't want the garlic to brown/burn. Add the white wine at this time to deglaze your pan, use a metal spatula to help get those essential brown bits up from the bottom of the pan. If you're using non-stick or Teflon pans do not use metal on them, do this step with a wooden spoon. Add the chicken stock and squeeze in the two lemon wedges. Simmer for 2 minutes, to burn off the alcohol.

Add your cooked pasta to the pan of chicken and sauce, mix thoroughly with tongs. Add the parmesan and toss so everything is coated evenly.

Plate in a nice sized pasta dish with more parmesan, parsley, and lemon wedges to garnish. I also served this entree with fresh cut bakery Italian bread from my local grocery store with Italian seasoned olive oil & butter, fresh broccoli, and peas as our healthy component!

From the Quarantine Kitchen of
Sandra Comerford

I am married and a mom of three children. Being a first-generation Italian, I loved watching my mom cook. I never took the opportunity to cook with her before she passed away. I always thought there would be more time. My fondest memory is of my home in Windsor Terrace, Brooklyn, NY. It was the home that always had an "open door policy." We literally never locked the door! My mom and dad were very poor in Italy. My dad came to America alone. He left his 13 siblings and parents. My mom came to America shortly after with her 3 siblings and parents. They prided themselves on having nice things. My dad worked hard so that my mom could stay at home and raise myself and my four siblings. Food was the no.1 priority in our home. I made a promise at my mom's funeral to make my home on Staten Island the new home with the "open door policy."

HOMEMADE CHICKEN CACCIATORE

INGREDIENTS

12 pieces chicken (thighs and legs)

Flour to coat

3 tablespoons olive oil

28 oz. San Marzano whole tomatoes

2 fillets of anchovies

1 onion sliced

15 oz. can black pitted olives, drained

15 oz. can chicken stock

12 button mushrooms, cleaned and quartered

2 tablespoons dried oregano

1 teaspoon crushed red pepper

Salt and pepper to taste

Season chicken with some salt.

Add seasoned chicken to Ziploc bag with enough flour to coat each piece.

Heat 1 tablespoon oil in oven proof, bottom heavy sauté pan and brown 6 pieces of chicken on both sides, making sure to shake off excess flour. This should take about 3 to 4 minutes per side (set browned chicken aside).

Heat 1 tablespoon oil and brown the remaining 6 pieces of chicken on both sides (set these aside as well).

Add anchovies and onions with another tablespoon of oil, saute until the anchovies completely melt.

Add mushrooms and stir for 2 more minutes.

Add tomatoes and stock, stir in oregano and crushed red pepper, cook for 2 more minutes.

Place the browned chicken in tomato mixture and add in olives.

Season with a few grinds of salt and pepper.

Cover and place in preheated 350°F oven for 1 hour, uncover and cook an additional 30 minutes. Serve over white rice and enjoy!

From the Quarantine Kitchen of
Giuseppe Donado

Every time my son and I see a Halal truck we have to stop and put an order in so we can take it home and taste it. We just love the spices that they use and the aromas that come from these trucks.

This quarantine has taught me to be more open-minded with different cuisines and making my own food. I also enjoy when my friends want to try those recipes and they let me know that their families enjoy it as well.

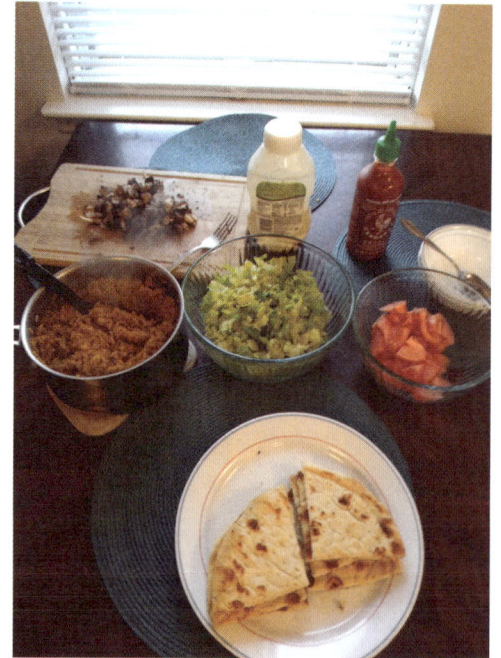

HALAL CHICKEN OVER RICE

INGREDIENTS

Chicken
(Make this in the morning so it can marinate)

2 pounds of boneless/skinless chicken thighs

2 tablespoons of oil

1 teaspoon of lemon juice

1 garlic clove (chopped)

½ teaspoon of dried parsley

½ teaspoon of dried oregano

½ teaspoon of cayenne pepper

½ teaspoon of black pepper

½ teaspoon coriander powder

2 teaspoons of Adobo seasoning

Mix well and refrigerate at least 2 hours or longer.

Rice
(Can double this up to make more rice)

½ onion (chopped)

2 cloves of garlic (chopped)

1 tablespoon of butter

1 cup of Basmati or Jasmine rice

2 cups of chicken or vegetable stock (or water)

1 teaspoon of paprika

1 teaspoon of tumeric powder

1 teaspoon of cumin powder

Pinch of salt

For white sauce (Make this in the morning so it can marinate)

½ cup whole-fat Greek yogurt
1 cup of mayonnaise
2 tablespoons of water
1 tablespoon of white vinegar
½ teaspoon salt
½ teaspoon black pepper
½ teaspoon or parsley
2 teaspoons of sugar
1 teaspoon of lemon juice

Mix well and refrigerate (Use a squeeze bottle to get same effect)

Cooking chicken thighs
Heat pan to medium-high heat, then add chicken thighs and cook 5 minute per side.

Flat bread
Warm up in the oven at 200°F for 5 minutes or warm in pan on very low at 2 minutes per side. (You can also use microwave or toaster oven).

Salad
Chop up lettuce and a medium tomato.

For red sauce (Make in the morning so it can marinate). Can also use Sriracha hot sauce instead of making this.

4 dry chilies
1 teaspoon of cayenne pepper
1 garlic glove (chopped)
½ teaspoon of salt
½ teaspoon of sugar
½ teaspoon of onion powder
½ teaspoon of black pepper
1 tablespoon of vinegar
1 tablespoon of lemon juice
1 small, plump tomato chopped

Blend together then refrigerate (Use a squeeze bottle to get same effect)

Cooking rice
Melt butter and add onion and garlic.

Add rice and toast over medium-high heat for 1 to 2 minutes.

Add chicken or vegetable stock (or water) and bring to a boil until you almost see the rice.

Reduce heat to very low and cover for 10 minutes.

Fluff up the rice, take off heat, and leave covered for another 5 minutes.

From the Quarantine Kitchen of
Lorie Strano

My favorite recipe growing up was my Aunt Nellie's fried chicken; you would walk into her house and smell the oil and you knew she was making her yummy fried chicken. In her high pitched Brooklyn, NY, accent she'd say, "have a seat at the table."

I remember just watching her in her apron frying a bunch of chicken, her hands filled with flour, and patiently waiting until she brought the chicken to the table. The best part was the crunchy outside. Every time I make this dish I picture those summer days at Aunt Nellie's house.

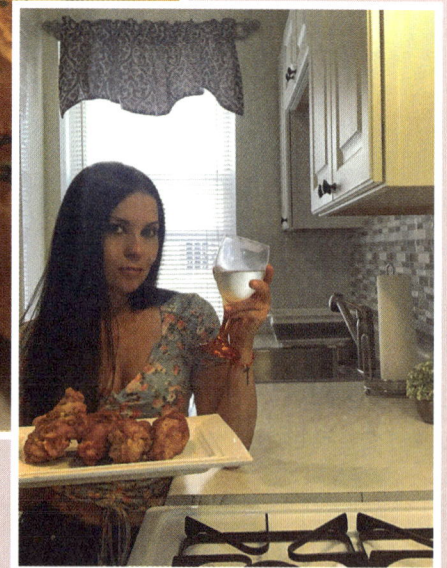

INGREDIENTS

6-8 pieces of chicken
(legs and thighs)

4 large eggs

1 teaspoon of garlic powder

¼ teaspoon of pepper

½ teaspoon of salt

2 cups of all-purpose flour

2 cups of canola oil

1 teaspoon of paprika

1 teaspoon of parsley
(for garnishing)

AUNT NELLIE'S FRIED CHICKEN

Rinse chicken in cold water, pat dry with paper towel.

In a large bowl add the eggs, salt, pepper, garlic powder. Whisk together.

Add the chicken to egg mixture (let sit for ten minutes).

In another large bowl add flour and paprika.

Coat all chicken in flour mixture. Shake off excess flour.

In a large frying pan, heat oil to 350°F. Carefully add the chicken to the pan, don't overcrowd.

Let cook about 6 minutes before turning. Turn chicken occasionally until golden brown.

When chicken is cooked transfer to a tray lined with paper towel.

Salt immediately while chicken is hot.

Garnish with parsley flakes.

Enjoy!

This recipe was handed down to me from my mom. As a child I would sit and watch her roll these heavenly bites of stuffed chicken. It was one of her many speciality dishes that I learned how to cook. Sadly, my mom passed away in 2013. I am grateful to have her recipe boxes full of delightful and scrumptious recipes. I will continue her legacy of cooking for my family!

JOANNE'S CHICKEN SPIEDINI

INGREDIENTS

4 pounds chicken cutlets (flattened to ⅛ inch thickness & cut into 2 x 3 inch strips)

2 cups seasoned breadcrumbs

1 cup grated parmesan

8 cloves fresh garlic (crushed)

Handful fresh parsley (chopped)

Salt & pepper (to taste)

1 packet Good Seasons Italian dressing mix (optional)

Olive oil (enough to moisten breadcrumbs)

1 stick butter (cut into small cubes)

1 block cheese (cut into small cubes, asiago, fontina, provolone, Swiss or mozzarella)

Combine breadcrumbs with grated parmesan, garlic, parsley, salt, pepper, Good Seasons mix, and olive oil. Mix well. Make it where mixture is moist, but not too oily.

Fill chicken strip with a spoonful of mixture, a cube of preferred cheese, and a dab of butter. Roll tightly and put on skewer.

When all done, drizzle each side of skewer with olive oil and pat with left over breadcrumbs.

Place on a sprayed baking pan. Put a dab of butter on top of each spiedini and bake at 375°F for about 12 minutes on each side or until chicken is cooked through.

Last, broil on high for 3 minutes each side until brown & crispy.

From the Quarantine Kitchen of
Roseann Turner

Thank you for allowing me to be a member of the Quarantine Kitchen. It has given me so much pleasure to cook so many of my recipes and share them with all of you!

I was also so happy to hear about the cookbook and that the proceeds would be going to the Stephen Siller Tunnel to Towers Foundation. My family and I ran that race a few years ago from Brooklyn to Manhattan. My son-in-law is a fireman. We all finished but it was tough, so this foundation is dear to my heart.

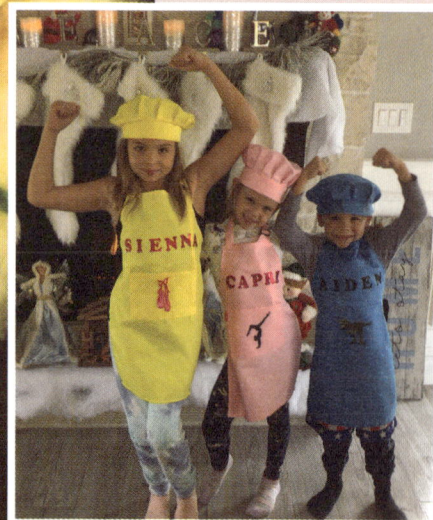

ROSIE'S CHICKEN FRANCAISE

INGREDIENTS

6 chicken cutlets pounded thin (place between 2 pieces of wax paper and pound with a mallet)

3 lemons

2 eggs, beaten

1 cup of sifted all-purpose flour

4 tablespoons olive oil

4 tablespoons butter for frying

½ stick butter for francaise sauce

1 (14.5 oz.) chicken broth

Salt

Pepper

Garlic powder

1 teaspoon flour for the sauce

Beat the 2 eggs. Season the chicken cutlets lightly with salt, pepper, and garlic powder. Place the cup of flour in a shallow plate. Dredge the seasoned chicken cutlets in the flour, then the egg mixture.

Add oil and butter to the pan and set to medium flame. Fry the chicken cutlets until browned on each side. Should look golden in color. Remove from pan, place in dish. Squeeze a little lemon on each. Cover with foil and keep warm.

When you have cooked all the chicken cutlets, clean out your pan and prepare the sauce.

Add a half stick of butter and melt. Add the can of broth and the juice of 1 lemon. Simmer for at least 10 minutes. Whisk in 1 teaspoon of flour to thicken a bit. Taste to see if you need more lemon.

Place the chicken cutlets back into the pan and warm through. Slice one lemon and place on each cutlet. Sprinkle parsley on top and serve. Enjoy.

During the quarantine, I would limit grocery shopping trips to once a week to be safe. I found smaller local grocery stores were better stocked and I was usually able to get chicken. Sometimes I found split chicken breast on the bone and other times it was boneless skinless chicken. Then there was a time that all the store had was chicken legs. This recipe is adaptable to each cut of chicken. I had eaten rosemary lemon chicken in the past. So, one night, I decided to try making it on my own. I had dried rosemary in my spice drawer, a big jar of chopped garlic in the fridge, and lots of lemons. My son loves everything lemon so I knew if I used lots of lemons he would eat it. My daughter and husband enjoy this dish, as well. My family doesn't always like the same dishes so this one is now something we have weekly.

Rosemary may be fresh or dried. Fresh garlic is best if you have it. If not, jarred chopped garlic works great and is easy. Lemon juice may also be fresh squeezed or one 4.5 oz. lemon-shaped bottles.

INGREDIENTS

2 pounds of boneless, skinless chicken breast

4 chopped garlic cloves

2 sprigs rosemary (separate from stem and chop)

⅓ cup olive oil

Salt

Pepper

Lemon juice from three lemons

LEMON ROSEMARY CHICKEN

Take chicken breast and pierce with a fork in multiple spots. This will allow it to absorb the marinade. Season with salt and pepper on both sides.

Place chicken in a Ziploc bag or container. Add olive oil to coat and allow some excess.

Add rosemary, garlic, and lemon juice.

Mix around the bag to make sure all the ingredients are spread evenly over the chicken.

Marinate in the fridge a minimum of 30 minutes and up to 6 hours.

Grill 10 minutes each side depending on thickness.

This dish can also be baked in the oven at 350°F for 30 to 40 minutes depending on the thickness of chicken.

Enjoy!

From the Quarantine Kitchen of
Renee Rohan Rappo

I am a special education teacher with the NYC Department of education for 21 years. I spent the quarantine remote teaching for a special education middle school inclusion program. It was overwhelming for me and my students. About a week in, I became sick with COVID-19 and it really knocked me for a loop but, fortunately, I was lucky and had a mild case. The great thing about quarantine was I was quarantined with my whole immediate family: my four adult children and two daughters-in-law, (all essential workers who had crazy work hours), my husband and two dogs, Pinot and Hazel. We are all grateful that we could be together and appreciate our love of family and food.

INGREDIENTS

8-12 chicken cutlets, pounded thin

¾ cup flour

¼ teaspoon salt

Pinch of black pepper

¼ cup grated cheese (parmesan or Locatelli)

6 tablespoons extra virgin olive oil

6 tablespoons butter

¾ cup of chicken stock

¾ cup dry white wine (Sauvignon Blanc or Chardonnay)

¼ cup lemon juice

¼ cup brined capers

Chopped fresh parsley for garnish

NO FAIL CHICKEN PICCATA

Rinse chicken and dredge in seasoned flour (flour, salt, pepper, and cheese).

Coat well.

Heat olive oil and 2 tablespoons butter in a skillet, medium heat.

Brown chicken cutlets for 2 to 3 minutes each side.

Remove from pan and place in a casserole dish in the oven at 250°F to keep warm.

Sauce
Prepare sauce in the same pan without removing any drippings.

Add stock, wine, lemon juice, and capers, and use a spatula to scrape drippings at medium heat.

Reduce liquid by half by keeping on heat and stir in remaining butter.

Pour over chicken and add parsley garnish.

From the Quarantine Kitchen of
Cole Maio

My name is Cole Maio. I'm 12 years old and have been cooking and creating really cool meals since I can remember. The earliest I recall is probably when I was about 6 or 7 years old. I started out with basic meals and then became interested in gourmet dishes. I think I'm pretty good at cooking, at least that's what everyone tells me! I've been playing football since the age of 5 and Lacrosse since I was 7. I love going bike riding in town with my friends, love playing video games, and especially love going to the beach and swimming in the ocean. I also do very well in school.

This year I'm graduating from elementary school with honors and awards and moving up to high school, which in my town is 7th through 12th grade.

I dedicate this recipe and all of my dishes to my parents and my sister. My father has a passion for cooking and has definitely passed that on to me. As much as my mother loves to cook and is good at it, my Dad and I usually take over in the kitchen! We cook with lots of love and excitement and I think that that is the secret ingredient that makes everyone happy.

I would like to add that my mother finished her treatment for breast cancer the day that the quarantine started. I've been helping with cooking for my family because I wanted her to have a break after being so strong through her recovery.

I hope you like my dish as much as we do!

CHICKEN VESUVIO

INGREDIENTS

8 chicken thighs, with skin

1.5 pounds of baby Yukon gold potatoes, cut in half

Kosher salt

Pepper

Vegetable oil

Fresh lemon juice

White wine (dry)

14 cloves of fresh garlic

Dried oregano

Dried thyme

Fresh parsley

Large roasting pan that covers 2 burners

Place potatoes in bowl with 1 tablespoon of vegetable oil, 1 tablespoon of kosher salt and toss to coat.

Trim the skin around the thighs so there is just enough to cover the top of the chicken. Pat chicken dry. Liberally coat both sides of chicken with kosher salt and black pepper.

Add 1 to 2 tablespoons of oil to roasting pan. Cook chicken skin side down over med/high heat until lightly brown and they start giving off some of their juices.

Add potatoes cut side down around outside of pan.

Sprinkle chicken and potatoes with 1½ teaspoons of dried oregano and ½ teaspoon of dried thyme.

Continue to cook for 8 to12 more minutes, constantly flipping and checking for golden brownness. Once done, flip skin side up.

Add 12 cloves of garlic to pan, cut in half the long way.

Add 1½ cups of white wine to pan (making sure not to pour over the crispy chicken skin).

Place in 450°F oven for 15 to 20 minutes until chicken internal temp is 185°F to 190°F.

In a bowl, mix 1 tablespoon of fresh lemon juice with 2 cloves of crushed garlic.

Remove chicken and potatoes from pan. Set aside.

Remove garlic from pan and blend to a fine paste. Return garlic paste to pan with the juices of the pan, and whisk well over medium heat until reduced and thickened.

Add the bowl of garlic lemon mixture and fresh chopped parsley to the pan and whisk to combine.

Plate chicken and potatoes and pour sauce over the potatoes and around the chicken (leaving top crispy).

Garnish with sprig of fresh parsley.

COOKED WITH LOVE. ENJOY!

I grew up in a Sicilian household, but my most favorite dish to eat is Coq Au Vin. I had it for the first time on my honeymoon in St. Bart's. I've been hooked ever since. I have zero patience for overnight marinaded meat, so I had to figure out a cheater's version for myself. (Most French recipes for this call for overnight marination of the chicken.) I would say the key to this recipe is chopping all the vegetables and having them ready.

Serve with roasted potatoes or mashed potatoes. I have also eaten this dish at restaurants served over egg noodles. Personally, I serve it over traditional Sardinian fregula pasta (sa fregula sarda).

I am sure you can do this in a crockpot and cook it all day and have it ready for dinner. I have never tried it that way.

INGREDIENTS

4 pounds chicken thighs
(I like boneless/skinless)

4 packages of 4 oz. diced pancetta
(you can substitute bacon)

Olive oil

A pinch of Kosher salt

Black pepper

16 oz. of mushrooms (if you don't use them, you'll have to add a quarter cup of water to the broth)

2 large shallots, chopped or ¾ of a giant yellow onion, chopped

6 oz. pearl onions, optional

6 stalks of celery, chopped

1 package of baby carrots

1 head of garlic (cut all cloves in half)

4 to 5 tablespoons of flour

1 bottle of dry white wine (or chablis)

1 cup chicken broth

1 cup of cognac or brandy

3 tablespoons dried thyme or 6 sprigs

1 to 2 bay leaves

3 tablespoons dried parsley or 6 sprigs

2 empty plates on side of stove for pancetta and chicken

VAL'S HONEYMOON "QUICK" COQ AU VIN

Preheat your oven to 350°F. Chop all vegetables and set aside. Clean chicken and set aside. Have pancetta ready and/or chop bacon, and put on the side.

Spray a large Dutch Oven or cast iron enamel pot with non stick spray. Add olive oil to cover the bottom, abut ¼ inch. Make oil hot.

Cook pancetta/bacon slices until golden and crisp. Medium heat. Remove them from the pot with a slotted spoon and set this aside in a dish.

Add a bit more olive oil to the pot. With tongs, brown each side of your chicken pieces, about 3 to 4 minutes per side. Do this in small batches. When you are done, put all the pieces aside in a large dish.

Add the mushrooms to the pot, continuing on medium heat. Brown the mushrooms until they are deep brown. (If you don't like mushroom skip this step).

Add the shallots, carrots, onions & celery. Cook until the shallots and onions are somewhat transparent. Add the garlic and cook for 2 to 3 minutes.

Add in flour and mix with the vegetables. You will see the broth starting to thicken. If the broth is still too watery after five minutes, add another tablespoon of flour.

Add ¾ of a bottle of wine. Mix and simmer. (Drink the other ¼ bottle of wine as you're cooking.)

Add in chicken broth and cognac/brandy and ¼ cup water (if you did not use the mushrooms). Bring all this to a simmer, lightly mixing.

Add in the browned chicken and the cooked pancetta/bacon & mix together.

Mix in thyme, parsley, bay leaves, salt, and pepper. (Don't add too much salt). Cook for about five minutes on the stove top, continually mixing. Cover your pot and put it in the oven for 2 ½ hours. (I like to mix the pot of food about an hour in.)

Enjoy!

FLO'S ALOHA SPARERIBS

In Memory of my Mom, Flo Vogt Svendsen.

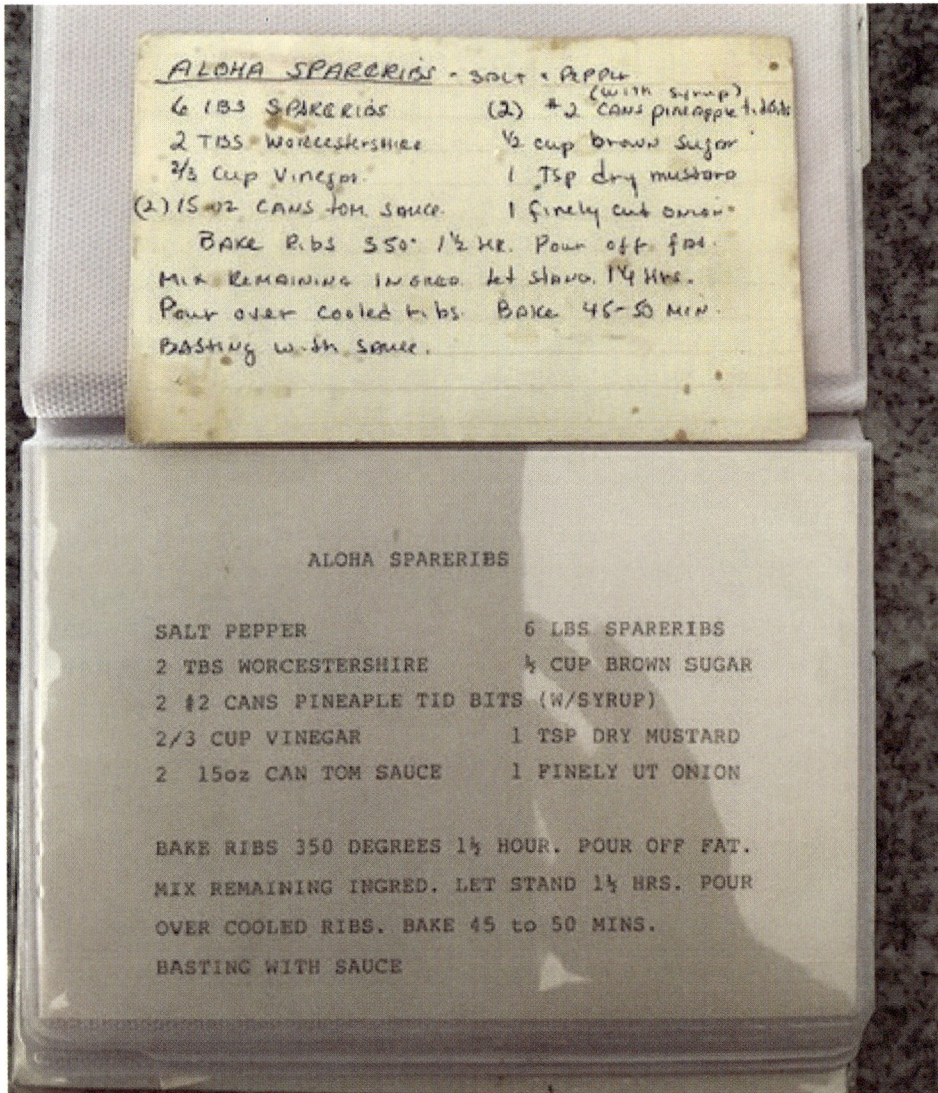

ALOHA SPARERIBS - SALT & PEPPER

6 LBS SPARERIBS   (2) #2 (with syrup) CANS pineapple tid bits
2 TBS Worcestershire   ½ cup brown Sugar
⅔ cup Vinegar.   1 Tsp dry mustard
(2) 15 oz CANS tom. sauce.   1 finely cut onion

BAKE Ribs 350° 1½ HR. Pour off fat.
Mix Remaining in gred. Let stand. 1½ Hrs.
Pour over cooled ribs. Bake 45-50 min.
Basting with sauce.

ALOHA SPARERIBS

SALT PEPPER   6 LBS SPARERIBS
2 TBS WORCESTERSHIRE   ½ CUP BROWN SUGAR
2 #2 CANS PINEAPLE TID BITS (W/SYRUP)
2/3 CUP VINEGAR   1 TSP DRY MUSTARD
2 15oz CAN TOM SAUCE   1 FINELY UT ONION

BAKE RIBS 350 DEGREES 1½ HOUR. POUR OFF FAT.
MIX REMAINING INGRED. LET STAND 1½ HRS. POUR
OVER COOLED RIBS. BAKE 45 to 50 MINS.
BASTING WITH SAUCE

From the Quarantine Kitchen of
Judy Sven

When I was growing up I wasn't a big meat eater but I remember my mom making these and enjoying them immensely. After she passed in January 2020, I was so excited to have found her recipe for my favorite meal.

My mom Flo was always creative "in making something out of nothing." She fed six kids on a very tight budget and worked full time. She was also a grandmother of 13.

Mom ran a successful marine business with my dad but people liked her food so much, she took over the small seaside restaurant in Blue Point, NY, on Corey Creek called the Anchor Inn (Now, JT's on the Bay).

My brother was a member of FDNY and my dad was a Captain in Bayport FD.

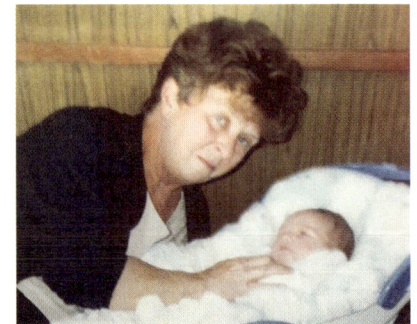

INGREDIENTS

Pizza dough (makes 8 small pizzas)

1 ⅔ cups water

1 to 2 teaspoons active dry or instant yeast

¼ cup olive oil

5 cups all-purpose flour

2 teaspoons salt

Arugula & Prosciutto Topping

5 plum tomatoes, diced

3 cloves of chopped garlic

Olive oil

Salt and pepper

Arugula

Mozzarella

Prosciutto

MARTARELLA'S GRILLED PIZZA

To make topping mix:

Mix all 5 ingredients in a bowl and set aside until you're ready to top pizza.

Add the mozzarella first and allow to melt.

Remove pizza from heat and add the mix with pieces of proscuitto.

From the Quarantine Kitchen of
Laura Gasparis Vonfrolio RN, PhD

It's been a difficult and stressful time for first responders during this coronavirus pandemic. Quarantine Kitchen helped me through the tough times as a stress reliever. Cooking is a therapeutic and creative activity as it makes one focus on the present moment. Using different recipes, I boosted my confidence and self esteem. It provided a great opportunity for family involvement in cooking different and interesting dishes and all enjoying a great meal!

My dad used to make this once a week, probably using leftover mashed potatoes and vegetables. During this time of quarantine it is always comforting to eat those foods that bring about great memories.

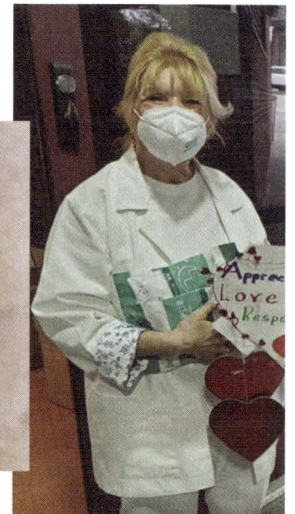

SHEPARD'S POT PIE

INGREDIENTS

1 pound ground beef

2 frozen pie crusts pre-made
(deep dish if you can find)

½ cup chopped red onions

1 clove chopped garlic

1 cup frozen mixed vegetables
(peas, green beans, corn, carrots)

3 potatoes

1 stick butter

Sautè chopped meat with onions and garlic. Set aside.

Boil potatoes, when done, mix with ½ stick butter. Set aside.

Sautè frozen mixed vegetables with ½ stick butter. Set aside.

Put chopped meat mixture in defrosted pie crust, then mixed vegetables, and then cover the top with the mashed potatoes.

Bake in oven for 30 minutes at 425°F.

From the Quarantine Kitchen of
Andrea Pollio

I was tired of making the same things for dinner every week. Being in quarantine, I started to make new things. I never made sausage and peppers before. Actually, I got this recipe from my newly married daughter who made it the week before me. My husband and kids love it. I double the recipe, add a hot sausage or two, and break out the Italian bread! Enjoy!

INGREDIENTS

6 links sweet sausage

2 tablespoons butter

1 yellow onion sliced

1 red onion sliced

4 cloves garlic, minced

1 green pepper

1 red pepper

1 yellow pepper

1 teaspoon dried basil

1 teaspoon dried oregano

¼ cup white wine

ITALIAN SAUSAGE & PEPPERS

In a large skillet over medium heat, place sausage and brown on all sides. Remove from skillet and slice.

Melt the butter in the same pan, stir in onions and garlic, cook for approximately 3 minutes. Put in sliced peppers, basil, oregano, and white wine. Cook until peppers and onions are tender. Add sausage, cover, and simmer on low for about 15 minutes until sausage is warmed up.

From the Quarantine Kitchen of
Diana Trabanco

We have a local country club in The Villages that has German night every Tuesday and we enjoy the pork schnitzel. When we were quarantined, I decided to replicate it and found this recipe. It is probably my new "go-to" dinner guest recipe. My husband raved about it and said it was better than the restaurant.

PORK SCHNITZEL

INGREDIENTS

4 boneless thin cut pork chops, pounded to ¼ inch thickness

1 cup all-purpose flour

3 beaten eggs

1 tablespoon Dijon mustard

2 cups Panko breadcrumbs

¼ olive or canola oil

6 tablespoons butter

2 teaspoons capers

2 tablespoons fresh lemon juice

Season the chops with salt and pepper.

Place flour in a plate.

In a bowl, mix together eggs and mustard. Place panko on a plate.

Dredge the pork in the flour, shaking off excess, then dip in the eggs and coat thoroughly with panko, pressing lightly to adhere.

Over medium heat, heat the oil in a large skillet.

Add 2 of the chops and cook, turning once, until golden on both sides, about 3 minutes on each side. Drain on paper towels.

Add more oil if necessary and do the other 2 chops.

Meanwhile, in another pan, melt the butter about 4 minutes, until browned. Stir in the lemon juice and capers.

Spoon the sauce over the pork and serve.

I like to serve it with buttered noodles and red cabbage–either Aunt Nellie's in a jar, or fresh using the recipe on the Dole red cabbage package, which adds apples to the fresh red cabbage.

From the Quarantine Kitchen of
Tracey Marino

The quarantine started on my daughter's 16th birthday. What a way to spend your Sweet 16. With my husband still working and my son still away at college, it was mostly my daughter and I at home. I wasn't really sure how my social butterfly was going to handle this quarantine between missing friends and missing school. She always enjoyed cooking and baking with me when she was a little girl, so after joining Quarantine Kitchen, I thought I'd get her back in the kitchen and we can cook together again. Our favorite dish from Quarantine Kitchen to make together is empanadas which I've never made before.

I decided to order this beautiful red casserole dish shown in the photo and told her when she has a family of her own she can take this dish and make her own memories then pass on to her kids and so on. My hope is that this red casserole dish will someday be used by my great-great-grandchildren and that this quarantine leaves her with some good, as we call it, "warm and fuzzy" memories knowing that I love her very "munch."

INGREDIENTS

1 box of Barilla oven-ready lasagna

6 sausage links (3 sweet and 3 hot)

3 cans Sclafani crushed tomatoes

1 tablespoon oregano

Bunch of fresh basil

3 cloves of garlic

One half of an onion

32 oz. container of ricotta cheese

1 large mozzarella cheese

2 eggs

Grated cheese

Black pepper

Olive oil

SAUSAGE LASAGNA

Preparation Directions

Sauce: Sautè 3 cloves of garlic in 3 tablespoons of olive oil. Add 3 cans of Sclafani crushed tomatoes, 1 tablespoon of oregano, handful of fresh basil, and half an onion (just throw half onion in and take it out when done). The longer the sauce cooks the better. I start my sauce the day before.

Decase 3 sweet and 3 hot sausage. Cook. Break apart, drain, and set aside.

Mix 32 oz. ricotta cheese with 2 eggs, grated cheese, mozzarella (I cube it but you can use shredded), and black pepper.

I used Barilla oven-ready (no boil) lasagna flat sheets (cuts down on the watery lasagna).

Now you layer. Sauce first, 4 lasagna sheets, some of the ricotta mix in a thin layer, sausage, sauce, grated cheese.

Repeat until you are left with your last layer of 4 shells for your top. Add remaining sauce, mozzarella.

Cooking Directions

Cover with foil and cook for an hour. When it's done let it sit for about 10 minutes before you cut it.

Two of my favorite kitchen tools to use when making this dish are my old wooden spoons to mix the filling and my cutting board.

When cooking this dish, the first thing that comes to mind is that it's a time-consuming dish to make. Pre-quarantine, I always cooked quick homemade meals.

From the Quarantine Kitchen of
Beatrice Montijo

Quarantine has given me a chance to spend quality time with my family. It has really allowed me to spend more time with my son. As a working mom, I missed many milestones as he was growing up. My son took an interest in cooking. He spent numerous hours in the kitchen helping me cook. This meant the world to me. It brought us closer. I have shared recipes and stories with him as a child myself in the kitchen with my mother before she passed on. Now he, too, will have great memories during this crazy, confusing time!

Cooking brings me happiness, peace, and a sense of calmness. The same has happened for my son. In quarantine, I've been able to make my favorite recipes like stuffed eggplant but also try new ones. Quarantine Kitchen has allowed me to see and try many of the wonderful recipes people have shared. Seeing my family's faces as I put a new dish on the table was priceless! Quarantine kitchen has kept my sanity. It has helped me feel connected to the outside world and discuss and review fun exciting recipes from others rather than focus on all the negativity. Thank you Quarantine Kitchen for helping me and my family during this pandemic.

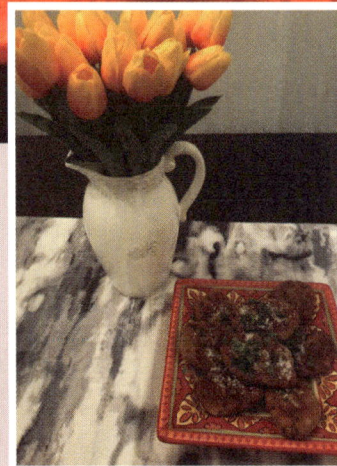

INGREDIENTS

1 medium to large eggplant

1 large egg, lightly whisked

1 large clove garlic, minced

½ cup plain breadcrumbs

½ cup, plus handful, parmesan cheese

1 tablespoon fresh basil, chopped

1 tablespoon fresh parsley, chopped

½ teaspoon dried oregano

Dash of salt

Dash of pepper

2 tablespoons oil in small bowl

Oil for frying (canola or olive)

STUFFED EGGPLANT (MELANZANE RIPIENE)

Wash and dry eggplant. Trim the top and bottom. Cut in half lengthwise and then each half into quarters. Should have 8 pieces.

Add eggplant with skin to a large pot of boiling water. Cooking on medium heat, stir frequently and gently, and make sure the eggplant is submerged in water. Cook for 20 to 25 minutes.

Drain eggplant in a colander and let cool completely. Once cooled, place eggplant in a large bowl and coarsely chop.

Add all ingredients (do NOT add oil), plus a handful cheese. Mix with your hands. The mixture should be dense, and not too firm. If the mixture is wet, add a handful of breadcrumbs.

Rub the palm of your hands with the oil from the bowl. This will help the mixture not to stick to your hands. Scoop some of the mixture into your palm and roll it as if forming a meatball. Then press mixture down, not too thin, and then form into an oval shaped patty, and then place on plate with parchment paper. Repeat process. When done, refrigerate patties for 1 to 2 hours.

Line a sheet pan with paper towels. In large skillet, heat about inch of oil. When oil is heated, place one eggplant patty at a time. Fry on one side until golden brown, on medium heat. Then, flip to the other side and fry until golden brown. Remove and drain on paper towels. Transfer to a platter, sprinkle with grated cheese and basil leaves.

Note: Can substitute dried herbs: ½ tablespoon basil and parsley. Eggplant mixture and/or patties can be made 1 to 2 days in advance. Can freeze on a tray and freezer bag; defrost before frying. Cooked eggplant can be eaten cold the next day, or heated up. Can be stored cooked, in Tupperware, for an additional 3 to 4 days.

From the Quarantine Kitchen of
Christina Tagliaferro-Gaitan

This was my absolute favorite thing to make during quarantine. It became my weekly tradition.

INGREDIENTS

For the dough:

4 cups all-purpose flour

1 tablespoon sugar

¼ teaspoon salt

1 ¼ teaspoons active dry yeast

1 ½ cups hot water

⅓ cup plus 2 tablespoons extra-virgin olive oil

For the pizza toppings:

My normal pie is fresh basil, homemade sauce, ricotta, shredded whole milk mozzarella.

CHRISSY'S FAMOUS PIZZA IN A PAN

Combine flour, sugar, salt, and yeast in a stand mixer using the dough hook. Combine the hot water and 2 tablespoons olive oil, then add to the mixer on low speed and mix.

Knead the dough with the mixer on medium-high speed until smooth about 10 minutes. Form a round ball of dough and flour your surface. Knead for another 5 minutes.

Pour the remaining olive oil into a sheet pan. Transfer the ball of dough to the pan, turning to coat with the oil. Cover loosely with plastic wrap and let rise in a warm place until the dough fills about two-thirds of the pan, 1 hour 45 minutes.

Stretch the dough and let it fit the entire length of the pan. Cover with plastic wrap for 30 minutes.

Easy trick: I make the sauce during the week, and I modify to use it for this dinner. I add Italian seasoning and tomato paste to thicken it up to a pizza sauce consistency. I also add garlic powder to the sauce. If you do not have sauce on hand, a local Italian specialty store likely will sell it ready to use.

Add toppings of preference.

The last step is the egg wash. This gives the pie a nice golden brown crust. To make my egg wash, I beat one egg with 3 cloves chopped garlic. Add 1 teaspoon of parsley flakes or an equal amount of fresh parsley. Season with salt and pepper. Egg wash the perimeter of the pie in entirety.

Bake at 400°F for 20 minutes.

From the Quarantine Kitchen of
Christina Tagliaferro-Gaitan

In the 1950's, this dish was a staple in my mom, Patricia's, home. The daughter of a Norwegian mother and Italian father, this one dish really defined the Norwegian heritage. It was the best meal for her to come home to after a long day at school or at work.

Mom passed the tradition down and made this dish a family favorite in our home growing up. We have many wonderful, warm memories having this hearty dish.

In 2019, I gave birth to my son and immediately following his birth had 4 months of hospitalizations. When I would get discharged, the first meal I would ask for her to make was this dish.

When the quarantine set in, I had to become creative when deciding meal options for my son. One day, while having mom's Norwegian meatballs, I nervously decided to mash one up and feed it to the baby. I wasn't sure what to expect, but needless to say, it was his first meatball and his favorite dish too!

INGREDIENTS

1 ½ pounds ground meatloaf mix

1 yellow onion diced very small

1 teaspoon salt

½ teaspoon pepper

1 egg, slightly beaten

2 slices bread soaked in milk

4 tablespoons butter

½ cup Gravy Master mixed with 3 cups water for gravy

Flour

Plain bread crumbs, if needed

PATRICIA'S FAMOUS NORWEGIAN MEATBALLS

Soak bread with milk in a bowl. Discard crust and excess milk, if any.

Add salt, pepper, onions, soaked bread, and egg to chopped meat. Mix well. If mixture is too soft to form meatballs add breadcrumbs a little at a time until you reach desired consistency. Place all the meatballs in a dinner plate.

Melt 4 tablespoons of butter in a deep frying pan over medium-high heat.

When the butter melts, add the meatballs all at once. (You might have to repeat if you have a lot of meatballs). Cook until browned on all sides. When browned add the water mixed with Gravy Master. Lower flame and cook meatballs in liquid for 15 minutes. Remove meatballs from liquid.

Mix flour with cold water until there are no lumps for the gravy. Add to liquid in pan until thickened.

Return meatballs to pan and simmer for an additional 5 to 10 minutes.

From the Quarantine Kitchen of
Prudence DiBello

Spiedini is a family favorite. This is a recipe passed down from Grandma Prudie. We guesstimated the recipe because we do it by look, texture, and taste. For as long as I remember, it has been our Easter tradition to get together and spend hours making these tiny delicious treats. During this quarantine year, my sister surprised me with a plate of the meat all sliced and we all made it in our own homes ... keeping the tradition going. A shout out to my EMT son, Joseph, and my soon-to-be front-line daughter, Jaclyn.

INGREDIENTS

8 pounds eye round (Should be semi frozen so that it could be sliced very thin on a slicer and then each piece pounded)

Filling

2 cans crushed tomatoes

2 cups breadcrumbs (maybe one plain and one seasoned)

½ cup breadcrumbs to sprinkle over top

1 cup grated cheese

½ small onion, diced

1 teaspoon salt

1 teaspoon pepper

2-3 tablespoons olive oil (two for first step – one to drizzle)

1 clove garlic, diced

MATRANGA FAMILY SPIEDINI

Chop onion very small and sautè in olive oil until translucent. Then, sautè garlic for a minute or two.

Add all ingredients; mix and cook for 5 to10 minutes and then let cool for about 5 to10 minutes. It should be the consistency of a soft cookie dough. Add breadcrumbs if necessary.

Each piece of meat gets approximately one teaspoon of filling, rolled in each piece.

Place each on baking pan and drizzle olive oil on top and then sprinkle breadcrumbs.

Bake on 375°F for 10 minutes. With spatula, flip them over and sprinkle a little more breadcrumbs. You can bake for another 5 minutes or turn on broiler and keep an eye on them for crispier spiedini.

GREAT GRANDMA ROSE BRAMAN'S BRISKET

From the Quarantine Kitchen of
Stephanie Goldberg-Glazer

Passed down by Annabelle Glazer to Andrea Glazer to Stephanie Goldberg-Glazer

INGREDIENTS

1 whole brisket (7-10 pounds)

2-3 large onions, chopped in large chunks

Brown sugar

Ketchup

Salt, pepper, garlic to taste

Preheat oven to 400° F. Spray roasting pan with cooking spray. Line pan with chopped onions. Season with salt, pepper, garlic. Place brisket bottom side up into pan. Season with salt, pepper, garlic. Cover meat with a thin layer of brown sugar and coat the sugar layer with the ketchup. Sear in oven for 15 minutes.

After 15 minutes remove pan from oven. Turn the meat over. Repeat the seasoning, sugar and ketchup on the right side of the brisket. Put back in oven for 15 minutes.

Reduce the oven temperature to 350°F. Cover the roasting pan tightly with foil. The brisket will release its own juices into the pan. Depending on weight of brisket, cook for 2 ½ to 3 hours. Check after 2 ½ hours. It is done when a knife inserted goes in easily with little resistance.

When the brisket is done, place the meat on a cookie sheet or other flat pan and cover to cool at room temperature. Let the liquid cool down to room temperature. Then using a stick blender, a food processor, or food mill, blend the entire mixture including the pan onions to make a rich gravy.

Refrigerate the meat and the gravy separately. After 8 hours or overnight, the brisket can be sliced and frozen with gravy in the pan (it can be reheated in same container). Reserve some gravy to be used to make the ever popular brisket potatoes.

INGREDIENTS

1 pound ground beef

1 pound ground pork
(Or you may substitute ground turkey, bulk Italian sausage, or mix and match 1 pound of each)

2 eggs

¾ cup Italian flavored bread crumbs
(If too much it will be dry.)

¼ cup parsley flakes or fresh chopped parsley

¼ cup parmesan cheese

1 tablespoon garlic powder

1 teaspoon Italian seasoning

¼ teaspoon salt (If using bulk Italian sausage, I omit the salt)

½ teaspooon black pepper

MY MAMA'S MEATLOAF, WITH A SPIN!

Put everything in a large bowl (I let it get to room temp) and mix with hands.

Shape and put in a loaf pan or baking dish.

Add 1 to 2 tablespoons ketchup, and a sprinkle of parmesan cheese on the top before baking at 350°F for 1 hour.

From the Quarantine Kitchen of
William Trang

The chef in my family is my husband, and we are so lucky that he loves to cook.

He was born and raised in France until he was 14 years old, where he was influenced and inspired to cook by his grandmother and mother, who both loved to do so. His mother is French, and his father is Chinese. Though his mother prepared traditional French dishes, she also broadened her cooking to include Asian dishes and other cuisines.

For the past 28 years we've been married, I can honestly say I may have cooked only a dozen times. Our kids are all grown: the oldest 25, the middle 23, and the youngest 21. Now more than ever, they truly enjoy and appreciate the creativity and variety of my husband's cooking. They show interest, are engaged, and ask questions. They too are starting to cook, especially my two boys.

By the time the shelter-in-place is over, I'm sure my kids will have learned some of my husband's culinary skills. Before the quarantine, we were empty nesters, and now we're back to a family of five. Our daily meals are the best part of the day, where we spend quality time and have conversations together. It unites us to enjoy the special meals prepared. I know that one day one of my kids, if not all three, will be a good chef just like their dad.

What better way to add joy and bonding time with the family than at meal time.

INGREDIENTS

3-4 pounds of beef

3-4 medium-sized carrots

1-2 medium onions

2-3 garlic cloves

Vegetable oil

½ cup ketchup

One packet of Kim Tu Thap oriental beef spices

Box (1 quart) of chicken or beef stock

Salt to taste

One long green hot pepper (optional)

Thin egg noodles or rice

Cilantro for garnish

Scallion for garnish

BEEF STEW OVER THIN EGG NOODLES

Cut beef into 1-2 inch cubes.

Dry rub beef with the packet of oriental beef spices, making sure all pieces are covered.

Cut onions into quarters and stir fry.

Add the dry rubbed beef, chicken or beef stock, ketchup, onions, and chopped garlic in a big pot.

Add water if all the ingredients are not completely covered.

Add salt to taste.

Boil on medium flame until meat is tender.

When meat is tender, cut carrots into 1-inch pieces, and add into pot. (Optional, add long green pepper for a spicier stew.)

Continue to cook on a low flame until carrots are cooked through.

The delicious stew can be served by itself or enjoyed over noodles or rice.

Lastly, sprinkle cilantro and scallion over the stew for garnish.

OUR QUARANTINE KITCHENS

SOUPS

Amazing soups were shared.

During the coronavirus quarantine, I have been finishing up an online Master of Arts degree in Learning with Emerging Technologies, which incorporates technology into teaching. As a music teacher, I am proud to say that I have been able to incorporate many new technologies into the instructional design of curriculum for online learning, especially now since we are all working and learning remotely. In addition, cooking and baking has become a pastime. Although I always enjoyed cooking and do so on a regular basis, the Quarantine Kitchen Facebook group has made it all the more so enjoyable in sharing recipes with other cooks and bakers.

I continue to pray for my essential worker husband and son during this pandemic. My husband is an MTA supervisor for New York City buses and my son is an officer with the New York Police Department. They are truly my front-line heroes!

INGREDIENTS

1 package of soup greens found in produce section (Typically includes: 2 celery stalks, 2 carrots, 1 parsnip, 1 turnip, 1 small onion, parsley, and dill.)

2 bouillion cubes (add 4 cups of water) or (2) 15 oz. cans of chicken broth

2 potatoes

(2) 6.5 oz. cans of unseasoned clam meat (or fresh from the fish market)

12 oz. can of evaporated milk or heavy cream

CLAM CHOWDER

Chop all vegetables and herbs and place in stock pot with boullion cubes and water, or chicken broth. Boil until vegetables are cooked (approximately 25 minutes).

Add clam meat and cook for about 6 minutes. Right before you are ready to serve, add the evaporated milk or heavy cream.

Add salt and pepper to taste. Serve with oyster crackers.

From the Quarantine Kitchen of
Malina Goodwin

I am so grateful to be quarantined with my amazing young son and husband. We were recently married in November 2019, and joke a lot about powering through these times in a newlywed phase, thank goodness!

As lots of people seem to be taking on their kitchen skills, we also love to cook and bake together. Classic quality time in the kitchen!

INGREDIENTS

Chicken or turkey breasts, bone-in

1 clove garlic, minced

½ cup onion, diced

½ cup carrots, diced

½ cup of celery, diced

Dash of your favorite seasoning

Fresh or freeze-dried dill

32 oz. chicken broth or stock
(lower sodium recommended)

1 bay leaf

1 package orzo (or pepe, or any
other favorite tiny pasta)

ORZO CHICKEN "STOUP"

Cover chicken with water and boil through (covered) on medium-high heat for about 45 minutes.

Remove meat to cool on a plate.

In same pot add the garlic, onions, carrots, celery, dill, bay leaf and broth/stock.

After removing skin and bones, cut or shred the meat and add back to the pot.

Cover and simmer for as long as you'd like.

Return to a boil and add entire package of orzo.

Lower heat to medium. Cover and cook through, stirring frequently until pasta has absorbed all or most of the broth.

Note: The soup recipe was my grandmother's. One time after accidentally dumping in all the pasta, the soup became all soaked up. It turned into a delicious stew, to my pleasant surprise (hence the inside joke of chicken "stoup.") The whole family loves it this way better!

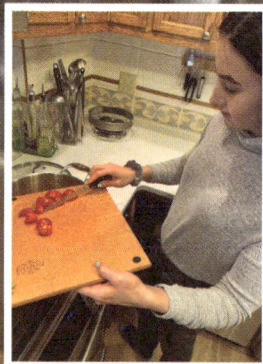

From the Quarantine Kitchen of
Elena DeCorato Brady
and Lauren Brady

The Molese people pride themselves on eating healthy meals with fresh ingredients typically grown in their garden. This lifestyle led to my maternal grandparents and great-grandparents' longevity. My Nonna, Carmela Ruggiero, lived until she was 88 years old, and her mother, my great-grandmother, Crescenza Pinto, lived until she was 96. This recipe and similar meal preparations served them well upon their arrival to New York during the Great Depression.

As Italian immigrants from Mola di Bari in 1935, meals consisted of pasta, beans, and vegetable scraps for flavor. This recipe is one of the best examples of the traditional meal that is also prepared on New Year's Eve by my sister, Camille Gallo, as a way of bringing good fortune in the new year.

CRESCENZA DECORATO'S LENTIL SOUP

INGREDIENTS

1 pound dry lentils, picked clean of any stones in the bag

2 dry bay leaves

4 cloves of garlic, finely chopped

2 cups celery, diced small to spoon size

2 cups carrots, diced small to spoon size

4-5 fresh tomatoes (canned is okay), diced small to spoon size

1 medium onion chopped

1 tablespoon salt

2 tablespoons basil (dry is ok)

¼ cup olive oil

½ small bulb of fennel (optional)

Yields 6 servings

After rinsing and sifting through the lentils, put the lentils in a 6-quart pot along with all the chopped vegetables, dry herbs, and olive oil. Fill pot with water 2 inches above the ingredients.

Bring the pot to a boil and then lower flame to simmer for 30 minutes.

Taste the lentils for firmness and when you're satisfied with the firm, but not al dente texture, your lentil soup is ready to eat!

We enjoy sprinkling some Pecorino Romano cheese on our individual bowls for extra flavor.

Buon Appetito!

From the Quarantine Kitchen of
Raffaella Pernice

Quarantine times!

Every morning we begin with one question: *What should we make today?*

Not only in my house, but across the ocean at my sisters house. Yes, they are in Italy but we keep in touch, plenty of 3 ways calls, and most days we decide what to make together, even if we don't agree on quantities of ingredients. As italian "un poco" can be between a pinch and a cup.

We are all home, everyone is staying in the kitchen, sometimes taking up my space. My son, Sal, is experimenting with different flours to make pizza dough. We have a pizza oven as part of our kitchen. My dauther worries about weight gain and unhealthy choices.

My husband is supervising it all. Between making pizza or soup, my feet are staying warm, thanks to my puppies.

Like a perfect marriage, this soup is the ideal combination of veggies and meat.

It will warm you up, and make you feel merry.

ITALIAN WEDDING SOUP

INGREDIENTS

Little meatballs:

½ pound of ground beef

1 egg

½ cup of bread crumbs

½ cup of Grana Padano grated

Minced garlic, black pepper

Pinch of salt

Soup:

1 carrot

2 cups of spinach

Mix all ingredients for the meatballs, and roll little ones.

On the side, warm up some water with a spoonfull of vegetable broth (optional).

As soon as the broth gets hot add the carrot slices, and the little meatballs.

Cook the meatballs and carrots in the soup for about 45 minutes to 1 hour, simmering.

Separetly, boil some rice or orzo pasta to add last minute to the soup, so it doesnt get soggy.

Add the spinach to the soup 2 minutes before serving.

Buon appetito!

From the Quarantine Kitchen of
Lisa Aragona

I decided to create my own version of chicken soup for a few reasons. One, is that I love soup and literally could eat it everyday! I've been making soup for my kids since they are born (they are 6 and 8 ½ and they love it too!). My mom always made soup for me and my brother growing up, too. However, when they moved to Florida, I needed to learn how to make it on my own. I started making it my mom's way and then over time, I developed my own way by puréeing in the vegetables and also using organic ingredients.

I come from an Italian family and we love to eat and cook. On top of that, I am a health coach and I truly believe food can be medicine as well, so we balance fun foods and healthy foods in my house! I try to find ways to keep our immune systems healthy and I truly believe that the version of my soup that I created has done just that! I have shared it with friends and family when sick and they swear by it as well!

I was invited to the Quarantine Kitchen page by a few friends. I was so happy to see so many familiar faces from both NY and NJ in the group! Being I love to cook, and live in my kitchen, and not to mention, I LOVE taking pictures of the dishes I make, I thought this page was perfect for me!
I posted multiple times a week and also contributed by posting on others amazing dishes as well. I loved having this group as a distraction during this time.

INGREDIENTS

1 organic whole chicken

7-8 organic carrot sticks

6-7 sticks of organic celery

2 organic yellow onions

4 cups of organic chicken stock

Pasta of choice

Grated Pecorino cheese

HOMEMADE ORGANIC CHICKEN SOUP

Place whole chicken in a pot with water on medium setting.

Cut up 2 celery sticks and 1 large onion and put into pot (you can add more if you like as well, this is just a guide).

Simmer on medium until the chicken starts to fall off the bone, and is soft.

Take chicken out and remove from bone. Place back into pot.

Add in 3 to 4 carrot sticks, cut up. (I don't add these until after so they aren't overly mushy.)

In a blender take 1 raw onion, 3 to 4 raw carrots, and 3 to 4 raw celery sticks with about 3 ½ cups water and purée them while raw (this holds the nutrients of the vegetable before adding to the pot which I feel is the key to boosting the immune system).

Add this into the pot with the already cooked chicken and broth that's cooking.

Add in 4 cups of organic chicken stock. (You can add more if you feel your broth started to dissipate.)

Let the entire soup mixture simmer between low and medium for another 10 to15 minutes. Add salt to taste.

Boil pasta of choice on the side. (For my picture and post I chose homemade tortellini.)

Garnish with Pecorino cheese to taste.

From the Quarantine Kitchen of
Connie Costa

This is a family favorite recipe loved by everyone especially my son, Mark Costa, Jr. He is in The U.S. Navy stationed in Japan. What I wouldn't give to serve him up a hot bowl of soup. Bravo Zulu Sailor. We are all so proud of you. Hoorah!

HOMEMADE FRENCH ONION SOUP

INGREDIENTS

4 large yellow onions

4 large Vidalia onions

1 tablespoon white sugar

1 tablespoon brown sugar

3 tablespoons butter

2 tablespoons extra virgin olive oil

2 cartons of beef broth

1 carton of beef stock

1 cup cooking sherry

1 tablespoon of herbs de provence or thyme or Italian seasoning (I use herb de provence)

1 ½ tablespoons of Better Than Bouillon roasted beef base

Salt and pepper to taste at the end. (Adding too much pepper to onion soup will make it bitter)

Slice onions thin.

In a large pot, put butter and extra virgin olive oil.

Once butter melts, add all the onions.

Start to sweat the onions. When onions start getting translucent, add the sugars; they will enhance caramelization. Cook, stirring until a nice rich brown. Add spices and sherry. Stir through and add all broth stock and Better Than Bouillon.

Cook on low, stirring occasionally.

When ready to serve, toast a baguette wedge with shredded mozzarella and gruyere cheese in the broiler. Top the soup with the baguette wedge and serve.

I was born in Taiwan and moved to the U.S. in 1973. My mother would make this for me as I was growing up in Baton Rouge, LA, and this is one of my favorite comfort foods. The tender beef and spicy broth is warm and inviting and I will eat it on a cold or hot day. My mother's is my favorite, but I love getting it off the street cart or these side pop up kitchens when I went back to visit Taiwan as an adult. I had a difficult time finding an "authentic" version that tasted as good as my mother's in any restaurant. The closest one I have found was at the Bellagio in Las Vegas at the Noodle restaurant. So, the only time I would have this soup is when my mother would come and visit me or when I visited her. She would always make me a large pot so I could freeze it.

I would never make this soup because I know it would never be as good as my mother's. With COVID and staying in, there wasn't much visiting from my mother for me to have this soup, since she lives in Tampa, FL, and I live in Chicago, IL. One day, I was missing her and I really wanted the soup so I called her and asked her for her recipe so I would think she was here making it for me. She said that I had to have a very particular Taiwanese bean paste (douban-jiang) to make it taste good. So she sent me a photo of it and I was off to the Asian store to get it as well as other ingredients.

INGREDIENTS

3 pounds of beef shank or chuck
2 tablespoons canola oil
(3) 1 inch ginger slices, smashed
1 bulb of garlic, smashed
4 scallions, sliced into chunks
1 onion, sliced
1 tomato, quartered
8 dried red chilies
3 tablespoons doubanjiang
   (spicy bean paste)
⅓ cup of soy sauce
⅓ cup of Shaoxing wine
1 teaspoon sugar
5 star anise
1 cinnamon stick
1 tablespoon fennel seeds
1 tablespoon cumin seeds
1 tablespoon coriander seeds
2 tablespoons peppercorn
1 tablespoon tomato paste
1 teaspoon five-spice powder
1 teaspoon black pepper
1 teaspoon white pepper
4 cups of beef broth
4 cups of water

Noodles (can use white noodles or ramen)

Garnish
Bok Choy
Cilantro
Scallions
Pickled mustard green

TAIWANESE BEEF NOODLE SOUP

Cut beef into 3-inch cubes. Put in a pot and cover with cold water. Bring the water up to a boil and boil for another minute until it foams up. Then, strain in a colander and rinse with water to remove the foam and grit.

Then, in cast iron pot or instant pot, add oil and sautè, ginger, star anise, cinnamon stick, fennel, cumin, and coriander seeds. Add tomato paste and sautè for a minute before adding onion, garlic, and scallions. Then add tomato and red chilies. Add the meat, bean paste, soy sauce, Shaoxing wine, sugar, five-spice powder, white pepper, and black pepper.

Then add beef broth and water. If you are using an Instant Pot, use the meat/stew setting. If you are using cast iron pot, get it up to a boil, and then simmer for 3 to 4 hours.

When you are ready to eat, boil noodles separately and then blanch the bok choy until tender.

When serving, fill each bowl with noodles, add beef and soup, garnish with bok choy, cilantro, more scallions, and chopped pickled mustard greens.

This recipe can be made in a cast iron pot or an Instant Pot.

OUR QUARANTINE KITCHENS

FROM THE SEA

"To do small things with great love."
~ Mother Theresa

1

2

3

4

5

6

7

From the Quarantine Kitchen of
Chef Guerrieri

Coming from an Italian family, baccala was a delicacy. Our most popular way of serving it was simply floured and fried. I lived in Portugal for about 16 years and cod became one of my favorite fish to work with. This beautiful, flaky, delicate texture is often avoided due to its "salty reputation." I'm a huge fan of dried cod, especially if I'm the one controlling the soaking. Dried cod tends to be salty when not soaked in water properly, but fresh cod is an entirely different category in my opinion, and easier to find. It's layered texture is a similar to that of Chilean sea bass and one doesn't need to worry if it was soaked properly. I saw many people sharing their family fish recipes and I wanted to bring light to a somewhat forgotten fish by simply giving an alternative to prepare cod. Especially a colorful and appealing recipe that is easy to prepare, easy to serve and that would easily tempt almost any palate. Most importantly, this recipe could be prepared with almost any fish filet if cod isn't available.

MEDITERRANEAN OVEN ROASTED COD

INGREDIENTS

6 filets of fresh cod
(or already soaked, dry cod)

12 to 15 small new potatoes
(halved, soak in water)

2 large onions (sliced thin)

10 to 12 ripe plum tomatoes
(cut into cubes)

Olive oil

Handful fresh basil
(washed and sliced)

1 cup pitted Gaeta olives

¼ cup capers (drained)

3 bay leaves

Bottle of beer

1 tablespoon butter

Preheat oven to 375-400°F.

Photo 1
Heat a good splash of olive oil and in a cast iron pot and place potatoes cut side down. Allow to brown on medium to high heat.

Photo 2
Add the onions and continue to cook until onions become soft. Season with salt and pepper. Add a good splash of beer and a tablespoon of butter. Reduce liquid to 50%.

Photo 3
Add the cut tomatoes and continue to cook about 10 minutes or until tomatoes become soft. Taste for seasonings, add dried herbs of your choice (oregano, herbs de provence, etc.). Mix well.

Photo 4
Add a good handful of fresh basil. Taste for seasonings. Remove from frying pan and put mixture aside in a bowl.

Photo 5
Pan sear the filet of cod on one side with olive oil in a non stick pan until brown and immediately place the cod into a baking pan big enough to hold the fish and the sauce. (Be sure to place the brown side up and the raw side down).

Photo 6
Place the sauce mixture with the potatoes allowing for the tops of the fish to be exposed (we want the fish tops to get crispy during baking).

Photo 7
Add the olives and capers on top spreading randomly. Bury the bay leaves under the sauce. Place in preheated oven for about 30 minutes or until the fish is slightly charred on top and the rest of the ingredients look perfectly baked (see finished photo).

I was born in Napoli, grew up in NY, lived in Lisbon and now back in NY. After 15 years of owning restaurants, I decided to consolidate them into a new concept called Smartwich. It was time to take white table cloth service and put the same quality between a hand made bread. Didn't take long for Smartwich to start gaining a delicious reputation. I soon opened a second location and was in the process of opening the third, but, like many other small business owners, I was forced to close my Smartwich shops during the caronavirus pandemic. I tested positive for the virus and things began to escalate; confusion, loneliness and fear set in. Feelings tend to multiply when our minds are not occupied, especially being forced to stay locked in our homes and your tv remote becomes your closest friend.

Quarantine Kitchen couldn't have come at a better time. It helped ease the escalation of my troubled thoughts that haunted me both present and future. I'm an extremest when it comes to being truly connected to food and after viewing profile after profile, just about everyone shared the same connection. I realized food was the familiar friend we all had in common. The QK group helped drown out so much of the negative and sad news we were being bombarded with day in and day out. The more I tuned into QK the more my mind was at ease and the closer I felt to being in "physical company " of others who simply loved to do what I love to do, cook! To me, and many others, this group became what we all call each other in restaurants because of all the time we spend together... a family.

The Quarantine Kitchen extends a very special thank you to Chef Guerrieri for his love and endless support on this amazing project. This journey has allowed us to meet some very special people. The Chef reached out early on to lend a hand, an ear, a spoon, whatever we needed! The funny thing is, we have not yet met him in person, this has all been virtual and via text/email, as Covid-19 would have it. We are looking forward to meeting our friend and one of our biggest cheerleaders in the very near future. We love you Chef!

~ Traci Cangiano

Chef Guerrieri says if you want to grill fruit try some of these...

Make sure the grill is SUPER hot and make these sauces to coat fruits before grilling; Remember when grilling fruit you want to get the outsides to get the charred taste of the grill without cooking the fruit all the way or it becomes baby food!

- Firm sweet apple wedges; mix lemon, honey, and finely chopped rosemary.

- Nectarine wedges or peach; melt some butter and toss with some cinnamon and chopped fresh sage.

- Semi green banana; purée some peanut butter in a blender with honey, any jelly, and balsamic vinegar. Coat the banana and grill.

- Thick lemon slices; put sugar, olive oil, and honey in a bowl and coat lemon generously before grilling.

- Cantaloupe wedges; lemon juice, honey, sugar, and fresh chopped thyme.

- Watermelon; cut nice pieces, use a chopstick to make a few holes and soak in port wine and sugar in a bowl before putting on grill.

From the Quarantine Kitchen of
Rose Angela Moore

My family and I love to eat good food! Most of my recipes come from Pinterest. It's a great place to keep recipes neatly organized and has incredible recipes and pictures. I can tell by just looking at a recipe how good or bad it will be. I feel that home cooking is very important to me and my family's health and well-being. We do not eat out a lot. I work full-time and cook dinner every night. I usually plan the menu for the week and mix it up to make it interesting. Once in a while we will eat out as a treat. So for me, this quarantine cooking is nothing new. My family background is Greek and Italian so those are my favorite recipes but I have learned to cook Spanish, Chinese, Mexican, Cuban, etc. I also love to bake. When I first got married at 23 I didn't know how to even boil water. I started watching cooking shows and bought cookbooks and I'm self-taught.

My family really looks forward to eating a good dinner every night. This makes me very happy.

INGREDIENTS

1 pound large or extra large shrimp, peeled and deveined

¾ cup fresh squeezed lime juice, 6 to 7 limes

¼ cup fresh squeezed lemon juice, 1 to 2 lemons

¼ medium red onion, finely minced

1 cup diced cucumber

2 chile peppers like serrano or jalapeño, deseeded and minced

2 tablespoons chopped cilantro

Corn Tostadas
Corn tortillas
Olive oil

Cuban Rice & Beans
1 tablespoon extra virgin olive oil

2 tablespoons tomato sauce (any brand)

1 teaspoon garlic, minced

1 teaspoon sofrito, store-bought is fine

2 packets Goya Sazón without annatto

1 packet Goya Sazón with coriander and annatto

1 can small red beans

1 ½ cups long-grain rice

SHRIMP CEVICHE WITH CORN TOSTADAS

Fill a pot with 8 cups of water and add 2 tablespoons of salt. This makes up a poaching liquid and helps to season the shrimp. Bring the water to a boil, add the shrimp, and then immediately take the pot off of the heat. Leave the shrimp in the poaching liquid until just cooked through, 2 to 3 minutes. You can tell when the shrimp is cooked when it's firm and opaque throughout.

Remove the shrimp from the poaching liquid and spread out on a cutting board to cool. When the shrimp are cool enough to handle, remove the tails (if there are any) and chop into bite-size pieces.

Add the cucumber, onion, minced chile peppers, cilantro, and chopped shrimp to a glass or ceramic bowl.

Pour over the citrus juices and a pinch of salt. Toss well, and then press the shrimp down into the liquid as much as possible. Cover and refrigerate for at least 30 minutes and up to 4 hours. Taste, and then season with salt if you feel it is necessary.

CONTINUED ON NEXT PAGE

SHRIMP CEVICHE WITH CORN TOSTADAS

CONTINUED FROM PREVIOUS PAGE

For Tortilla
Preheat oven to 425°F.

Lay the corn tortillas on a parchment paper-lined baking sheet and lightly brush both sides with olive oil.

Bake the tortillas for 5 minutes and then flip them over and continue baking another 5 minutes. The tostadas should be brown and crispy. Set the pan aside to cool

Rice Directions
Heat oil in medium saucepan over medium-high heat. Add tomato sauce, garlic, sofrito, and Sazon, cook until fragrant, about 1 minute.

Transfer liquid from can of red beans to measuring cup; add enough water to measure 3½ cups. Add liquid to pot; bring to boil. Add beans and rice; stir. Bring rice mixture to a boil; reduce heat to medium low and cook, covered, until water is fully absorbed, approximately 20 minutes.

Remove rice from heat. Let sit until rice becomes tender, 5 minutes. Fluff with fork before serving.

From the Quarantine Kitchen of
Rose Angela Moore

Classic Margarita and Guacomole to be paired with Shrimp Ceviche with Corn Tostadas.

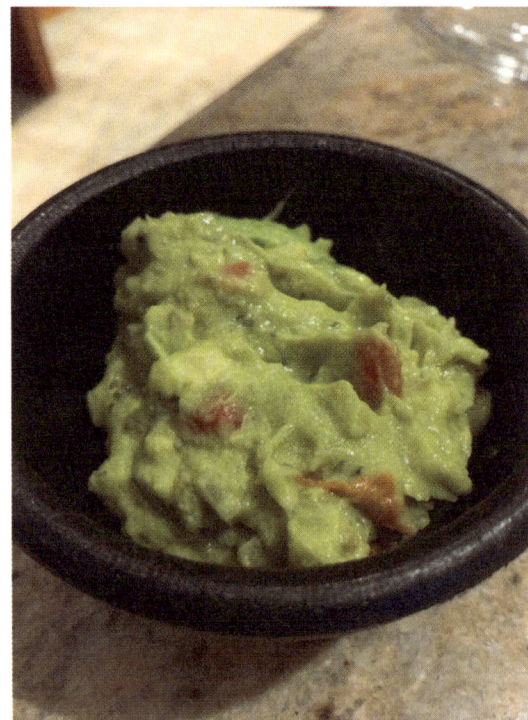

CLASSIC MARGARITAS AND GUACOMOLE

INGREDIENTS

Classic Margaritas

Kosher salt (for serving)

½ thick lime wheel (for serving)

2 oz. tequila

¾ oz. fresh lime juice

¾ oz. simple syrup

Guacamole

3 avocados

Red onion chopped (about ¼ cup)

2 cloves garlic minced

½ bunch cilantro leaves chopped

1 jalapeno finely chopped (or to taste)

1 large tomato or 2 smaller tomatoes, diced

1 lime juiced

4-5 shakes green Tabasco sauce

Kosher salt to taste

Fresh cracked pepper to taste

Margarita Preparation

Place some salt on a small plate. Rub rim of an old-fashioned or rocks glass with lime (reserve for serving); dip in salt. Fill with ice and set aside.

Combine tequila, lime juice, and simple syrup in a cocktail shaker. Fill shaker with ice, cover, and shake vigorously until outside of shaker is very cold, about 20 seconds.

Strain cocktail through a Hawthorne strainer or a slotted spoon into reserved glass. Garnish with lime wheel.

Guacamole Preparation

Pit avocados and mash in a bowl.

If you like your guacamole kind of chunky (that's how we like it), coarsely chop with the side of a fork instead of using the fork to mash it straight down.

Carefully stir in remaining ingredients until well mixed. That's it!

Creating meals keeps me connected to my daughter.

Ever since I was a little girl growing up in a Roman Catholic household, Easter week was celebrated with the traditional dishes. As a young girl, I have always enjoyed watching my parents cook and admired how much they placed an emphasis on cooking with the freshest ingredients. Carmine and Teresa Foresto are from Naples, Italy. They came here in 1960 to open their own restaurant. I grew up surrounded by different foods and delicious flavors that allowed me to become more cultured in the culinary world.

After countless hours of observing my parents at work in the kitchen, observing how they blended ingredients together and arranged meals in visually attractive presentations, I decided to take matters into my own hands and put my skills to the test. Over the years, my skills have adapted tremendously, which have allowed me to cook the most delicious meals that are appreciated by my friends and family. One family recipe that I hold dear to my heart is

Cozze and Vongole alla marinara, known here as mussels and clams, a delectable seafood dish made in a marinara sauce, which is a tradition passed down from my parents. We share this meal in my home on Holy Thursday.

When I got married, I hosted Christmas, Easter, and Thanksgiving holidays in my home with my husband, our four children, and extended family. Cooking and hosting brought everyone together at the dinner table and sharing a meal meant bonding time, nurturing, and a good way to express my creativity with the people I love most.

Last August, I suffered an insurmountable and devastating loss. My 24-year-old daughter, Alexandra, was caught in a rip current while on vacation with friends in Mexico. While immersed in mourning my daughter, the world was faced with a silent killer, the coronavirus. The fear of losing another family member paralyzed me.

Cooking keeps my mind occupied and my heart spiritually connected to my daughter. She was the one child that especially loved Mom's cooking. Her memory is alive with me in the kitchen.

One day while scrolling through Facebook, I was invited to join a group called Quarantine Kitchen, where people cook and share their meals during this fearful time. The idea truly intrigued me and I accepted the invitation. I thought, *I love to cook, therefore, why not participate?* The first post consisted of dishes I had already cooked the week before. The response was overwhelming! The group not only gave me the opportunity to showcase my cooking, but also a feeling of camaraderie. It has provided me the distraction I needed from my sadness and sorrow. It gives me great joy to share my culinary prowess with the world at this time. I am honored to be part of the Quarantine Kitchen!

CLAMS AND MUSSELS MARINARA

INGREDIENTS

3 pounds mussels debearded, scrubbed and rinsed thoroughly

2 dozen little neck clams

1 large onion, finely chopped

4 cloves of garlic

1 cup of good quality white wine

1 teaspoon tomato paste

1 can plum tomatoes

Parsley and basil to finish

Heat olive oil in in a sauté pan over medium heat. Add onion, garlic and red pepper flakes. Add tomato paste. Add mussels and clams to the pan. Turn up heat and cover. Once clams and mussels are opened, add the white wine and reduce, add plum tomatoes. Cooking time no more than 10-15 minutes. Finish with fresh parsley and basil. This dish can be served with either bruschetta for dipping or pasta.

My name is James Paone, Director of Operations at The Italian Cultural Foundation at Casa Belvedere. I am third eldest of 11 children born to my parents, Ralph and Rosarita Paone. Growing up in a large Italian family on Staten Island, NY, life revolved around food. From the daily meals, to entertaining and holidays, there was always a focus on what we are going to eat.

My mother, who emigrated from Naples, Italy at 16 years old, was my inspiration to cook. She was able to transform anything from our pantry into a gourmet meal. Learning to cook didn't start in the kitchen, but in the market. Shopping with mom was like a lesson in purchasing produce, seafood and meat, always with a budget in mind. My cooking skills were further honed by my favorite Food Network TV stars Emeril Lagassee, Molto Mario, Alton Brown, and Gida Delorentis. My children, Rosemary and Sophia, now 21 and 24, were my sous chefs. We would spend hours together in the kitchen or watching our favorite cooking shows.

I am very proud that my daughters enthusiastically embraced a love for cooking. Like I did with my mother, we enjoyed spending time together shopping and cooking. They, too, branched into other areas as their interests grew beyond my knowledge. But nothing can replace the traditional holiday dishes that were passed from my mother to me and now to them.

Christmas Eve was a sacred holiday in our family. As kids, we would joke that our future spouses would have to sign a prenuptial agreement that stated spending the Christmas Eve holiday with our family was non-negotiable. As our family grew, we all took on the responsibility of making a traditional dish or two. My dishes were smoked eel, octopus salad, and calamari salad.

In today's world, it's almost impossible to get everyone together for Christmas Eve, including mom's 30 grandchildren. We do our best to get everyone under one roof, and spend quality, joyous time together while we feast on our traditional dishes.

Quarantine Kitchen was a great outlet for me to share my culinary skills with the rest of the world. It was also the catalyst to preparing my favorite Christmas Eve seafood dish, calamari salad. As my post said, why do we seem to make our favorite holiday dishes only once a year? My post was well-received and it opened a dialogue with many group members who shared their holiday stories (and dishes).

INGREDIENTS

2 tablespoons sea salt

2 ½ pounds calamari, bodies and tentacles

1 cup fresh parsley, chopped

2 lemons

1 cup Spanish olives, chopped

¼ cup brining liquid from olives

3 cloves fresh garlic

1 teaspoon red pepper flakes

1 cup celery, sliced

⅔ cup olive oil

Sea salt and pepper to taste

CALAMARI SALAD

Bring large pot of water to boil, add 2 tablespoons sea salt to water. Slice calamari bodies into rings. Place calamari into boiling water; boil for approximately 2 minutes until calamari are somewhat firm, but tender.

Drain calamari and set aside.

Place remaining ingredients to a bowl.

Add calamari to bowl and mix well. Add salt and pepper to taste.

Allow to marinate 2 hours, best if overnight.

May want to squeeze additional lemon and add salt and pepper to taste if marinating overnight.

From the Quarantine Kitchen of
Rosemarie Garcia

My name is Rosemarie and I am a mother of five from Brooklyn, New York. I truly love cooking for family and always put my heart and soul into it. My daughters often help me in the kitchen and together we create new and fun delicious recipes.

Quarantine Kitchen has given me something to look forward to during this pandemic and I am truly grateful to be a part of this group. Being able to share my recipes, food pictures, and receive inspiration from fellow member posts has been wonderful during this time.

On that note, I'd like to share my family's favorite summer dish ... my "Zesty Shrimp Stuffed Avocado." It is light, refreshing yet filling.

Thank you Quarantine Kitchen for creating such an inspirational group.

INGREDIENTS

4 ripe avocados (8 servings)

Rice
2 cups of long grain rice
1 teaspoon of salt
½ tablespoon of canola oil
4 cups of water

Creamy zesty sauce
2 tablespoons of red onion
2 tablespoons of yellow pepper
2 tablespoons of red pepper
2 tablespoons of orange pepper
2 tablespoons light mayonnaise
2 tablespoons of plain Greek yogurt
  or sour cream
Juice of ½ a lemon
Juice of one orange
¼ teaspoon of salt
¼ teaspoon of pepper
¼ teaspoon of chili powder

Cilantro lime dressing
½ cup of cilantro
2 garlic cloves
¼ cup of red wine vinegar
¼ cup of extra-virgin olive oil
Pinch of salt
Pinch of black pepper
Juice of 1 ½ limes

Shrimp
3 cups frozen shrimp
¼ teaspoon salt
¼ teaspoon of cumin
¼ teaspoon of paprika
¼ teaspoon chili powder
2 garlic cloves minced
½ teaspoon of extra virgin olive oil
Juice of 1 lemon

ZESTY SHRIMP STUFFED AVOCADO

In a medium-size pot, add your olive oil and then rice. Cook on low to medium heat, stirring consistently for about two minutes. Now add water and salt and give it a good stir. Turn heat to high and let cook until the water starts to bubble, almost to where you can see the rice again. Once this happens turn to lowest heat, cover, and allow to cook for about 25 minutes.

Remove the shells and clean and devein your shrimp. In a medium-sized bowl, add your shrimp, salt, cumin, paprika, flakes, chili power and minced fresh garlic. Then add your lemon and olive oil and mix well. Place a piece of plastic wrap and let marinate in the refrigerator for about 20-30 minutes.

Dice red onion, yellow, red, and orange pepper and place in a medium-sized bowl. Now add mayonnaise, yogurt or sour cream, lemon juice, and orange juice. Finally, add salt, pepper, and chili powder and mix together evenly and set aside.

In a large skillet, cook shrimp on medium-high flame for about 1 minute on each side until ends start to turn brown, but not burning them. Remove and set aside to cook for about 10 minutes.

In a blender or food processor, add your cilantro, garlic, red wine vinegar, olive oil, salt, pepper, and lime juice. Blend and set aside.

Chop up the completely cooked-down shrimp into small pieces and add to creamy zesty sauce. Give it a good stir until mixed evenly.

Take the ripe avocados and slice down the middle, separating into two. Remove the skin and use a knife to hack out the pit. Slightly spoon out a bit of the avocado from the middle, making the center a bit wider. Scoop shrimp in the creamy zesty sauce and top with cilantro lime dressing. Pair with a side of rice, some tortilla chips, and garnish with some cilantro.

From the Quarantine Kitchen of
MaryAnn Sciametta

My husband and I had a house down the Jersey Shore. We would bring our five children there in the summer. We would go crabbing off our pier or off our boat and collect bushels of crabs. We would leave a trap in overnight and by morning we would have a good amount of crabs. We would freeze them alive in brown paper bags. They stay fresher this way. We had crabs for the whole winter. Until this day, we still go crabbing during the summer and continue our tradition.

Being home during this pandemic was a struggle because I couldn't be with my family and I missed my grandchildren. I love to cook and bake so finding this Quarantine Kitchen page on Facebook was a lifesaver during this pandemic. There are some fantastic cooks in this group and I'm grateful to all who have shared their recipes.

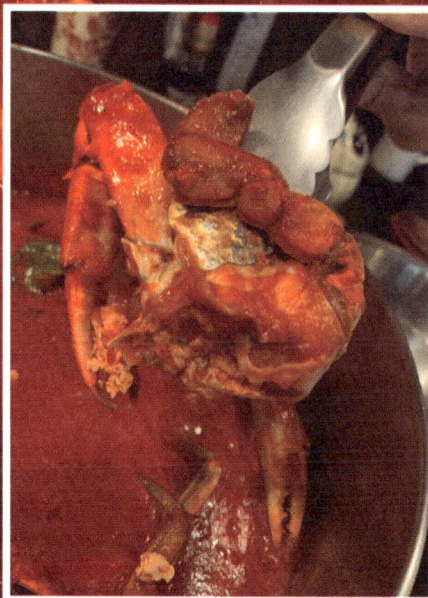

INGREDIENTS

1 dozen crabs – cleaned & cut in half

3-4 tablespoons extra virgin olive oil

4 garlic cloves (minced or pushed through a garlic press)

6 oz. can tomato paste

(4) 28 oz. cans crushed tomatoes

6 fresh basil leaves
(more, if you prefer)

2 teaspoons of salt

1 teaspoon black pepper

2 pounds spaghetti

CRAB SAUCE

Clean crabs very well and cut them in half so they are easier to turn in the pot.

Sautè crabs with garlic and oil until they start to turn red, on a low flame.

Then, add the tomato paste and continue to sautè the crabs.

After the crabs are partially red, add the cans of crushed tomatoes.

Bring to a slow boil and then down to a simmer.

Continue to turn the crabs periodically.

Add salt and pepper (to taste).

Add basil.

Cook pasta in salted boiling water until al dente (firm to the bite).

Strain pasta and return to pot, adding sauce.

Serve crabs in a separate bowl.

Bon Appetit!

CLAMS & SPICY GARLIC LINGUINE

Bring large pot of lightly salted water and clam juice to a boil. Add the pasta and cook, stirring occasionally, until al dente.

In large nonstick skillet, heat butter over medium heat. Add the onions, basil, oregano, crushed red pepper, and garlic. Reduce heat to low, cook for 5 minutes and add the extra virgin olive oil. Add the clams last and cook for 5 minutes.

Pour over pasta. Season with sea salt and pepper, and garnish with fresh basil.

Enjoy!

From the Quarantine Kitchen of
Stacey Ahmad

I starting making this when I first met my boyfriend Ron. We both love seafood but he loves this dish because is spicy and has a lot of flavor. Now this is our stay-at-home "dining out" meal.

INGREDIENTS

Bag of frozen clams or fresh

1 pound linguine

4 tablespoons of butter

1 large red onion, finely chopped

10-12 garlic cloves, minced

2 tablespoons chopped fresh basil

2 tablespoons dry oregano

1 tablespoon of crushed red pepper flakes, or more to taste

1 cup of extra virgin olive oil

Sea salt and freshly ground pepper

Bottle of clam juice

From the Quarantine Kitchen of
Debra McCue

INGREDIENTS

5 pounds frozen calamari, defrosted and strained well. Remove the tentacles, clean well.

For the sauce

3 to 4 garlic cloves (crushed)

Olive oil

(4) 16 oz. cans crushed tomatoes

(2) 16 oz. cans crushed tomatoes with puree

2 tablespoons of dried oregano

5 to 7 leaves of fresh basil

2 tablespoons paprika (paprika is Nanny's secret ingredient to give rich color and flavor)

Salt and pepper

For the stuffing

48 oz. Italian seasoned breadcrumbs (approximately 2 containers of 24 oz. breadcrumbs)

Olive oil (approximately ¼ cup)

Cold water

NANNY'S STUFFED CALAMARI IN RED SAUCE

This recipe was used as one of the seven fish dishes served on Christmas eve for twelve people.

Remove the cartilage and clean the insides of the bodies using your index finger, keeping the calamari bodies intact. You can also purchase frozen and already cleaned calamari, but be sure the package includes the tentacles.

Marinara Sauce Preparation

In a large saucepot, heat a good splash of olive oil and add the garlic cloves until golden. Immediately add all the sauce and allow it to come to a boil, stirring occasionally. Add the remaining ingredients. Taste for seasonings and simmer.

Stuffing Preparation

In a large bowl, add the breadcrumbs. Using a wooden spoon, gradually add the olive oil as you mix. Gradually add cold water until the consistency is a soft but loose stuffing mixture. It's okay to use a little extra olive oil. Taste for seasoning.

While the sauce is simmering, place the stuffing in a pastry bag or create a "stuffing funnel" using parchment paper. Fill each calamari body with the stuffing leaving an inch at the end to close with a toothpick. Try to "weave" the toothpick in order to get a tight seal. Repeat. Once all the tubes are stuffed, gently place stuffed calamari tubes and the tentacles into the sauce. Continue to cook over low heat for approximately 30 to 45 minutes or until the calamari is super tender. This will depend on the size of the calamari.

From the Quarantine Kitchen of
MARIA MANNINO-VERIKAKIS

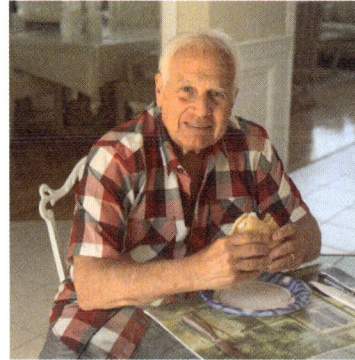

This dish is extremely special to me! It's my father's favorite meal. He discovered adding the shrimp to it during a very trying time in our lives while my mother was recovering in the hospital. Eating out a lot while he was staying close to the hospital in NYC, he frequented a tiny hole-in-the-wall pizza place that made this dish called *Linguini Sinatra.* Yes, named after the beloved singer with blue eyes. Of course, my father ordered this because it combined his two favorite things: Frank Sinatra and linguini and clam sauce.

Over the years, I created this version. I hope you enjoy making it for your loved ones as much as I do. Being part of Quarantine Kitchen has been the silver lining of a very trying time in our history! I can't thank the founders and the organizers of this cookbook enough for giving us solace and a safe space to come together to share our love for cooking. I will always think fondly of the interactions I have had on Quarantine Kitchen and will always appreciate the distraction from Covid-19 and negativity on social media. QK is a place where strangers, of all races, ethnicities, backgrounds, and differences have come together in unity to just share our love of food. Putting all those differences aside and enjoying each other's company, sharing recipes and tips, giving compliments, and asking questions. This page, that started out as just a sharing recipe group to help us all figure out what to cook each night, has meant so much more to me. It has given me hope for a better tomorrow and that the world is still good and we can all get along in spite of our differences.

LINGUINI SINATRA

INGREDIENTS

Bushel of Little Neck or Cockle clams

½ - 1 pound of jumbo shrimp, cleaned and cut in half or thirds

Olive oil

Lots of Garlic (8-12 cloves)

Fresh parsley

Salted butter (about ½ a stick)

Good white wine (I use Pinot Grigio)

1 lemon (juice & zest)

8 oz. bottle of clam juice

Salt and pepper

Red Pepper flakes, optional

Linguini

Marinara sauce to make it pink or red, optional

Clean clams including shells because this recipe is cooked with the clams in the shells. I soak clams in a bowl or pot so they have a chance to spit out any sand, this can be done until water is clean without any sand.

Sauté chopped garlic in olive oil in a large deep skillet or pot until garlic is browned. Add butter, salt, pepper, and hot pepper flakes if using. (If making red or pink, this would be when you add the marinara sauce) Once butter is melted, add your clams.

Once clams are in pot, pour white wine over the clams. I usually use ½ to ¾ of the bottle. Squeeze lemon juice over clams and zest too. Add the clam juice. Give everything a nice mix and add parsley.

Cover pot or pan, let simmer on low and allow the clams to open.

In a separate frying pan, sauté cut up shrimp in olive oil and garlic if you like it garlicky. Cook until pink and add a little white wine too and/or lemon juice.

Cook pasta until al dente. Pour clams over pasta and then top with cooked shrimp. Sprinkle with more chopped parsley and enjoy!

Mangia Bella!

From the Quarantine Kitchen of
Terry Marie Tulli

This has been my family's Christmas Eve dinner for more than 40 years with all fresh fish and spices. I learned to cook this from my mother-in-law along with my mom and dad by my side. My mom had been helping with this until three years ago when she passed away. When my mother-in-law passed away 10 years ago, it became all hands on deck as we usually have 24 people for dinner. We continue the tradition of preparing this meal for our family; we usually start to cook & clean 2 days prior to Chirsmas Eve, as the sauce is always better after it sits and marinates. We clean all the fish and store in containers and plastic bags. Since we are so many people and the recipe is tripled, I use 2 roasting pans for the sauce and then add the fish 1 hour before we sit down to dinner.

Quarantine Kitchen has made a very difficult time for everyone enjoyable with all the delicious recipes that we shared and continue to share.

Hope you enjoy my recipe and God bless us all!

INGREDIENTS

3 cans crushed tomatoes

1 can tomato paste

2 tablespoons olive oil

2 tablespoons fresh parsley

2 tablespoons fresh basil

2 tablespoons minced onion

2 tablespoons crushed red pepper

5 cloves crushed garlic

2 teaspoons oregano

2 teaspoons pepper and salt to taste

2 pounds large or extra large cleaned shrimp - devein and remove tail

2 pounds sea scallops

2 pounds calamari

2 - 3 pounds of 3-5 oz. lobster tails

24 little neck clams

24 New Zealand mussels

1 can scungilli

Spaghetti, linguini, or bucatini - your choice

SEAFOOD FRA DIAVOLO

In extra large walled pan, add paste,1 cup of water, and all spices to sautè approximately 10 minutes on low heat and stir continually. Add 3 cans of crushed tomatoes and cook for about 1½ hours. Season with more spices to your taste.

Scrub and rinse the clams and mussels, then put in a pot with about 1 cup water and steam them until they open. Remove shellfish and rinse with hot water. ** Discard any that don't open. **

Clean calamari also by running under cold water and removing the mucus.

Depending on the size of the lobster tails you use, you can cut them in half as I always do. Also remove the fins if necessary.

Add all the seafood to the sauce approximately 1 hour before eating and simmer on low in order to not overcook the fish. I do not precook any of the fish as it cooks enough in the sauce and you don't want it rubbery.

Boil water for the pasta and cook for approximately 8 to 10 minutes unitl al dente. Add pasta to the large walled pan and mix or place in an extra large platter/bowl and place seafood on top of pasta.

Garnish with more parsley.

Note: You can cut down on the fish and add any fish of your choice, which I have also done. In addition, I have used frozen fish and dried spices for quicker preparation time for dinner.

Dinnertime is paramount in our home. We pray, eat, laugh and enjoy each other. I joined Quarantine Kitchen because I felt there was an outlet of people who had a similar interest, cooking, and we could all take ourselves away for a bit from what was going on in the world. Many people, I'm sure, in this group were directly affected or know someone that was affected from being an essential worker that has had fears of going out and getting sick, to losing a job, trying to figure out school at home or even the most tragic, facing the death of a loved one or dear friend.

Cooking is therapeutic for me. It allows me to decompress from the day. It gives me satisfaction that I can feed my family and bring them together. That's my secret … bringing people together. As far back as I can remember, the smell of food in my home always gave me a feeling of comfort and love. My Sicilian mom is a major part of that feeling of love and comfort in my life, and cooking together with her and being able to eat together with my sister and she brought our days together, and until this day keeps us together. We still Facetime video our dinners and compare recipes down to my Sunday sauce. I am happy to have become part of this internet "family" of cooks. Quarantine Kitchen has made a family in some way of all these people who are members who may never have crossed paths in their life. It's funny but wonderful that we were able to share our photos and stories of ancestral recipes, etc. Thank you Quarantine Kitchen for being an outlet to just step away from our tough reality of this pandemic for a bit.

JOSIE'S
QUARANTINE KITCHEN
EST. 2020

INGREDIENTS

**1 pound of linguine pasta
(pick your favorite brand)**

**1 pound small fresh or 1 bag frozen
deveined and unshelled shrimp**

**Fresh or dried parsley
(if dried, use at least 2 tablespoons)**

**Red pepper flakes
(at least 1 teaspoon, add more if
you like spice)**

At least ½ cup of chicken stock

3 cloves of minced garlic

½ cup of Panko breadcrumbs

2 large lemons

½ cup of shredded parmesan cheese

4 tablespoons of softened butter

Olive oil

Salt

Black pepper

Bring a large pot of water to a rolling boil and once the water starts to boil, add at least ½ tablespoon of salt and mix.

Zest lemon in a bowl, add at least 1-2 tablespoon of oil and half of the minced garlic as well as half of the parsley. Save the rest for later. Rinse fresh or defrost and rinse shrimp and lightly towel pat dry and add to the bowl. Add a pinch of salt and red pepper flakes, mix together to allow to marinate a bit and set aside.

In a large pan, melt 2 tablespoons of butter and add Panko breadcrumbs and a pinch of salt. Stir the breadcrumbs until they become golden brown just about 3-4 minutes. Once you see them get to a golden color, remove from heat and set aside in a bowl.

Add linguine to boiling water and allow to cook until al dente, 9 to10 minutes. Make sure to taste-test a strand to your liking, cook longer for softer pasta. Once pasta is done, make sure to reserve 1 cup of pasta water for later, drain the remaining water.

In the same large pan used for breadcrumbs, melt 1 tablespoon of butter on high heat and add shrimp. Cook for at least 4 minutes until opaque in color. Squeeze juice of one lemon on shrimp. Once cooked, remove and set aside on a plate.

Wash large pan and then melt a tablespoon of butter. Add rest of garlic until golden brown. Add parsley, chicken stock, and reserved pasta water. Cook until fragrant and then add in shrimp and pasta. Add a pinch of salt and black pepper. Add the parmesan cheese and squeeze juice from the second lemon over the whole prepared pan of food. Buon Appetito.

Pour yourself a glass of white wine and enjoy!

OUR QUARANTINE KITCHENS

DESSERTS

Sweets were the most popular things to make
in our kitchens, all sorts of amazing sweets.

DANI'S BLUEBERRY CRUMB PIE

INGREDIENTS

Ingredients for Filling

1 pie crust

5 ½ cups of fresh blueberries

½ cup of sugar

⅓ cup of flour

1 tablespoon cornstarch

1 tablespoon lemon juice

2 tablespoons water

Ingredients for Crumb Topping

1 cup of flour

1 cup of light brown sugar

1 stick of softened butter

Thaw pie crust, if frozen. Preheat oven to 400°F.

Combine blueberries, sugar, flour, cornstarch, lemon juice, and water in a large bowl.

Line a pie pan with crust. Fork holes in bottom of crust for air.

Pour in blueberry filling.

In a bowl, mix crumb topping ingredients with a fork until large crumbs form. Sprinkle crumbs on top of blueberry filling.

Place pie on lined baking sheet and bake for 25 minutes. At 25 minutes, cover sides of pie with foil so crumbs don't burn. Keeping the pie in the oven, turn the temperature down to 375°F.

Bake for an additional 30 to 45 minutes.

Cool pie for 3 hours before serving.

INGREDIENTS

5 tablespoons brown sugar

6 tablespoons sugar

4 tablespoons butter softened

2 teaspoons vanilla

3 tablespoons whole milk

¾ cup flour

½ teaspoon salt

½ cup chocolate chips
(or more to taste)

KRISTINA'S FROZEN EGGLESS COOKIE DOUGH

In a bowl, mix brown sugar, sugar, and butter until combined.

Add in vanilla and milk and mix.

Gradually stir in flour.

Add salt and mix.

Mix in chocolate chips.

Roll mixture in a log and cut into small pieces.

Freeze for 1 to 2 hours or until ready to use.

Enjoy!

We all tried the Impossible!

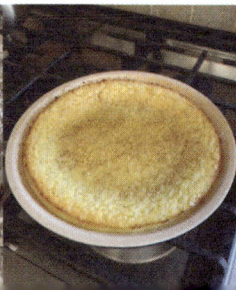

In Loving Memory of Roberta Smith

From the Quarantine Kitchen of
Tracey Dedee

Submitted by Tracey Dedee on behalf of her mother, Roberta Smith.

When Roberta was just a young child in the 1930's, her mother was diagnosed with Tuberculosis (TB). She spent the majority of Roberta's life in and out of facilities under quarantine before passing away. Roberta's mother's illness left her father, as the sole provider for the majority of Roberta's life. Fondly, Roberta would often recount the time when her family lived above a bakery, where her father worked as a baker for a period of time.

Thankfully, the love of baking carried over to Roberta. She made delicious pies with incredibly flaky crusts for her family. However, one of her most memorable pies was Impossible Pie, which formed its own crust. This simple, coconut custard-like pie was, and still is today, a family favorite.

Sadly, Roberta passed away on June 7, 2018, at the age of 86, but her love for her family lives on through her delicious recipes.

IMPOSSIBLE PIE!!

Here's what's cookin': **Impossible Pie**

Serves: **6**

Recipe from the kitchen of **Roberta Smith**

kissin' wears out cookin' don't

Put in blender in order listed:

- 4 Eggs
- 1/2 Cup Flour
- 3/4 Cup Sugar
- 1/2 Cup Soft Margarine
- 1 Tsp. Vanilla
- 2 Cups Milk
- 1 Cup (or less) Coconut

Beat one minute — Bake 45 Min. 350° (9" Pie Plate)

There isn't much of a story behind it. I have always had friends who were restaurant owners, chefs, and bakers (majority of them from Italy). I never cared for cream puffs because I wasn't a big fan of the filling. So after watching them make them, I knew how to make the puffs, then I just experimented myself to make a cream that I liked. And it's an easy cream and recipe where anyone (whether experienced or not) would be able to make them. But the puff itself has to be followed exactly as the recipe says or they will not fluff. Enjoy!

DIANA'S FAMOUS CREAM PUFFS

INGREDIENTS

Ingredient for pastry puff:

½ cup water

½ stick of butter

½ cup sifted flour

2 eggs (if doubling up, use 3 eggs)

Ingredient for cream filling:

1 cup heavy cream

1 cup milk

1 box of instant French vanilla pudding

Few drops of vanilla extract, optional

Directions for Filling
Place all ingredients in a bowl and mix. Then place in refrigerator until it thickens.

Directions for Pastry Puff
Preheat oven at 400°F.

Melt butter with water over medium heat in a pan (stovetop). Once melted, add flour and mix until it becomes a ball. ONLY USE A WOODEN SPOON TO MIX. Let cool for 5 minutes. Mix one egg at a time until fully mixed.

Spoon dough into balls on baking sheet and check after 15 minutes. Once top starts to brown, take puffs out of oven. Let puffs completely cool. Once cooled, you can cut the tops off and fill with cream. Sprinkle a little flour on top and place in the refrigerator.

Being quarantined for the better part of two months hasn't been all that bad. I live downstairs from my parents, so they're happy I'm home. Spending time with my husband, bingewatching our favorite shows, we wouldn't normally get to do during normal work weeks. Our dogs are confused, yet happy, that we're home, as well. We're using this time to tackle a few home projects that were put on hold. My dad and I have cooked many different dishes and desserts. We've all laughed at just about everything to keep our sanity and we have movie night once a week.

This recipe was handed down over the decades from Aunt Bunny. She would make them for every occasion and holiday.

INGREDIENTS

10 graham crackers made into crumbs

8 oz. bag semi-sweet chocolate chips

½ cup chopped walnuts, optional

1 cup shredded coconut

14 oz. can condensed milk

Stick of butter

13" x 9" glass pan

CHOCOLATE CHIP GRAHAM BARS

Preheat to 350°F.

Place whole graham crackers in a Ziploc bag and crush them up with a rolling pin

Melt the stick of butter and mix with the graham cracker crumbs. Spread evenly at bottom of pan.

Use a 1/4 of the condensed milk and pour evenly over graham cracker crumbs.

Spread the chocolate chips around evenly, then walnuts (if using), then the coconut. Pour remaining condensed milk over top, evenly.

Bake in oven for about 30 minutes for metal pan, 40 minutes for glass pan.

Cool, cut into squares, and enjoy!

From the Quarantine Kitchen of
Malina Goodwin

My son always takes such pride in his baking. As a true chef does, he relies only on the feedback of his tasters. He doesn't even eat his own creations! He was already like that before the quarantine, so naturally a favorite pastime during it was to expand his creativity in the kitchen. While we had so much fun creating together, he took my role as his sous chef seriously (perhaps a little too much at times!) Good thing he wasn't watching the TV show "Hell's Kitchen" one Gordon Ramsay is enough!

CHOCOLATE CAKE LOAF

INGREDIENTS

10 tablespoons butter

1 ¾ cup all-purpose flour

½ teaspoon baking soda

1 ½ teaspoons baking powder

1 teaspoon salt

½ cup dark cocoa powder, sifted

½ cup light brown sugar

1 cup sugar

3 eggs

2 teaspoons vanilla extract

1 cup heavy cream

Preheat the oven to 350°F. Grease a loaf pan with baking spray.

In a medium saucepan over medium-low heat, melt the butter until smooth. Set aside and allow to cool.

In a large bowl, combine the dry ingredients: flour, sifted cocoa powder, baking soda, baking powder, sugar, light brown sugar, and salt. Whisk until fully incorporated.

In a separate bowl, whisk the eggs. Add the remaining wet ingredients and beat until smooth.

Mix the wet ingredients with the dry ingredients, and mix until there are no longer any clumps of flour.

Transfer batter to loaf pan and smooth out the top using an angled spatula. Don't fill the pan all the way, leave at least 1 inch from the rim of the pan so it doesn't overflow.

Bake for 45 to 50 minutes, or until a toothpick inserted in the center comes out mostly clean. Allow to cool for 10 minutes.

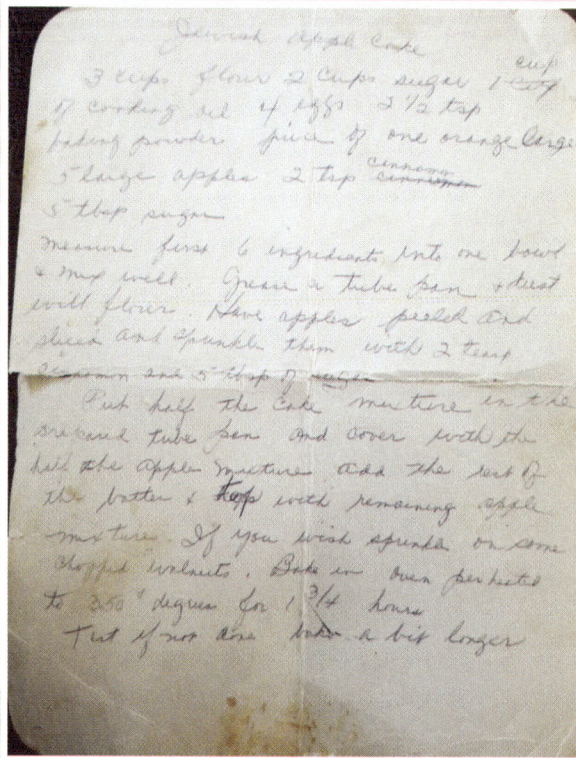

Jewish Apple Cake

3 cups flour 2 cups sugar 1 cup
1 cooking oil 4 eggs 2 1/2 tsp
baking powder juice of one orange large
5 large apples 2 tsp cinnamon
5 tbsp sugar

measure first 6 ingredients into one bowl
& mix well. Grease a tube pan & dust
with flour. Have apples peeled and
sliced and sprinkle them with 2 teas
cinnamon and 5 tbsp of sugar

Put half the cake mixture in the
second tube pan and cover with the
half the apple mixture add the rest of
the batter & top with remaining apple
mixture. If you wish sprinkle on some
chopped walnuts. Bake in oven preheated
to 350° degrees for 1 3/4 hours
Test if not done bake a bit longer

From the Quarantine Kitchen of
Theresa Panarella

Grandma Nettie was my mother's mom. She was so loving, kind and generous and was the most phenomenal cook I have ever known. She loved feeding everyone and taught me to make home-made manicotti, chicken cacciatore, eggplant parmigiana, her prized pizza rustica (I've been making it for 33 years, with my sisters, daughters, nieces and granddaughters) and several baked goods. I've actually enclosed a picture of her and my grandma Florence (my dad's mom) putting together her delicious manicotti. I attribute my love of cooking and baking to both my mom and grandma Nettie Bettie! She was my grandma and my close friend. We shared a love of cooking and she patiently taught me all her family secrets.

I actually enclosed another picture of Grandma's recipe written on a piece of cardboard in her handwriting. Yes, I still have several of her recipes that she actually hand wrote.

She was loved and will be missed by all who were blessed to have known her. I'm grateful to have had such a wonderful grandmother and role model.

I hope you'll enjoy this cake as much as my family does and smile thinking of this beautiful loving woman who fed every-one her delectable food, even everyone in the beauty parlor where she went. (She brought pans of homemade eggplant parmigiana very often to them on Saturday mornings!)

GRANDMA NETTIE'S JEWISH APPLE CAKE

INGREDIENTS

3 cups all purpose flour

2 cups of sugar

1 cup of canola or vegetable oil

4 eggs

2 ½ teaspoons baking powder

Juice of 1 large orange

5 large apples, peeled, cored, and sliced thin

2 teaspoons cinnamon

5 additional tablespoons of sugar

Measure first 6 ingredients into a bowl and mix well. Grease and flour a bundt pan.

Sprinkle apples with the 2 teaspoons of cinnamon and 5 tablespoons of sugar.

Pour half the cake mixture into the pan and cover with half the apples. Pour the rest of the batter on top of the apples and top off with the half remaining apples.

Optional: You can add some chopped walnuts on top before baking.

Bake in preheated oven at 350°F for 1 1/2 hours.

After the cake was cooled I added a vanilla glaze that consisted of powdered sugar, vanilla extract, and milk.

Buon Appetit!

From the Quarantine Kitchen of
Theresa Muszel

While being quarantined due to the coronavirus and unemployed, I started to clean out my pantry and while doing this I found an old newspaper recipe clipping. A close friend of mine had submitted a crumb cake recipe that goes back three generations. I called my friend Carlet, and I decided to give the recipe a try.

CRUMB COFFEE CAKE

INGREDIENTS

For the cake:

¼ pound butter, softened

1 cup of sugar

2 eggs

⅔ cups of milk

2 cups flour

1 teaspoon vanilla extract

For the crumbs:

1 ¼ cups of flour

¾ cups of sugar

¼ pound softened butter or margarine

1 tablespoon cinnamon

Heat the oven to 350°F. Grease a 9x13 inch pan. In a large mixing bowl cream together ¼ pound of softened butter, 1 cup of sugar, and 2 eggs. Beat on medium speed until light and fluffy. In the same bowl, mix alternately the 2 cups of flour, ⅔ cups milk, and 1 teaspoon vanilla. Mix thoroughly and transfer into the baking dish.

For the crumb mixture that will go onto the top of the cake: Mix 1 ¼ cups flour, ¾ cups sugar and a ¼ pound of softened butter or margarine, and 1 tablespoon of cinnamon. Mix up with your hands. Hold the crumb mixture and squeeze gently to shape the crumbs and drop on top of the cake mixture.

Bake 40 minutes until lightly brown. You can test by inserting a tooth-pick or knife into the center of the cake. If it comes out clean it's done. Cool for 10 minutes. Sprinkle the top with powdered sugar. ENJOY!

From the Quarantine Kitchen of
Laura Aldrich

Early into our marriage many years ago, I discovered my husband was not a traditional birthday cake kind of guy. He preferred the cheesecake his mom used to make and thus, a birthday tradition was born. This no egg, no bake recipe is a creamy mixture of goodness—sweet, yet has a lemony smooth texture that is enveloped by a no bake homemade cinnamon graham cracker crust. One of my favorite earlier pictures is my husband and our son teaching his son on the fine art of batter licking! Now almost 40 years later, you can see my husband STILL loves his batter ... and cheesecake on his special day!

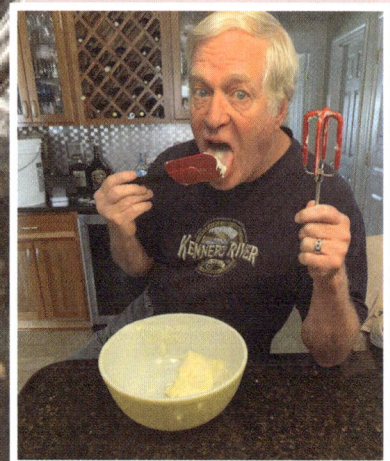

INGREDIENTS

No Bake Graham Cracker Crust

For an 8-inch pie dish
1 ⅓ cups (or use 9 whole) graham crackers, crushed

¼ cup brown sugar

¼ teaspoon cinnamon
(for more of a cinnamon taste, add more to your liking)

¼ cup butter, melted

For a 9-inch pie dish
1 ½ cups graham crackers, crushed

⅓ cup packed brown sugar

1/2 teaspoon cinnamon
(more if you like)

⅓ cup butter, melted

4 Ingredient No Bake Cheesecake
8 oz. package cream cheese, softened

14 oz. can sweetened condensed milk

⅓ cup lemon juice

1 teaspoon vanilla

Graham Cracker Crust
Blend the crushed graham crackers and brown sugar together. Add cinnamon. Mix well. Pour in melted butter and mix thoroughly. Set ⅓ cup aside. Place the rest in the pie plate and press firmly. Pour cheesecake on top and smooth out. Sprinkle reserved crumbs over top.

Filling
In medium bowl, beat cheese until light and fluffy. Add sweetened condensed milk and blend thoroughly. Stir in lemon juice and vanilla. Pour into crust. Chill 3 hours or until firm. Refrigerate leftovers.

From the Quarantine Kitchen of
Denae Jenkins

This cake recipe was passed down by my son Kevin Moss's Grandma Gloria Brown, from his father's side of the family, and it's now part of my family tradition when we all get together for the holidays. I make this pound cake for Easter, Thanksgiving and Christmas ... it's very rich, thick and delicious. It goes great with vanilla ice cream. Grandma Brown is 96 and lives in Florida.

GLORIA BROWNS' CREAM CHEESE POUNDCAKE

INGREDIENTS

2 sticks of margarine

1 stick of butter

8 oz. package of cream cheese

3 cups of sugar

7 eggs

3 cups sifted flour (1 ½ cups all-purpose flour and 1 ½ cups cake flour)

1 tablespoon vanilla extract

1 tablespoon lemon extract

Combine first 3 ingredients, beat well with heavy duty mixer, gradually add sugar, and beat until light and fluffy, about 5 minutes.

Add eggs one at a time, beat well.

Add flour gradually.

Stir in vanilla and lemon extract, beat well.

Pour batter into well greased 10-inch tube cake pan.

Bake at 325°F for 1 hour and 30 minutes until cake test done.

Cool in pan 10 minutes, remove from pan and cool completely.

From the Quarantine Kitchen of
Tracy Bodoni

My name is Tracy Bodoni and I live in Sewell, New Jersey. March 12, 2020 was my 49th birthday. I went to work that day and received flowers from my daughter and my boyfriend. I decided to take them home at the end of the day just in case we couldn't go back to the office because of this mysterious virus that everyone was talking about. On Friday, March 13th, my company made an announcement that everyone was to begin working from home effective immediately in order to help stop the spread of the COVID-19 virus. The next day, severe anxiety set in; I have asthma, my parents are in their 70's, and my 26-year-old daughter had just started her nursing school clinical at a hospital. The days, weeks, and months after that day all seem like a blur.

My friend Lisa told me about the Quarantine Kitchen page because she knows that I love to cook and bake (and posting the photos to Facebook!). At first I thought it was just photos of kitchens so I posted a photo of mine, but then I realized it was so much more than that! It was also beautiful photos of food–breakfasts, lunches, dinners, snacks, appetizers, cakes, cookies, etc. from all different cultures and backgrounds. We all gathered in one place and had the same things in common–our passion for cooking and baking and our love of food! I have always posted pictures of my food for as long as I can remember, but now there's a place we can all go to get ideas, exchange recipes, get inspiration, and some much-needed positivity during very uncertain times. We have all been quarantined to our homes and summoned to our kitchens, so why not make the best of it? I've made some great food, a few new friends and have been inspired in so many ways.

My favorite recipe is a made-from-scratch chocolate cake that my mom received more than 50 years ago from her friend's grand-mother. This recipe is by far the most-made recipe in my family. My mom made it for my Dad and I until I started baking and making it for my own family. Now I make it for their birthday, my daughter's birthday, and a million other occasions! This recipe is very special to me and it will always remind me of my mom and how she inspired me to be the cook and baker that I am. I am also very grateful that we still get to bake together.

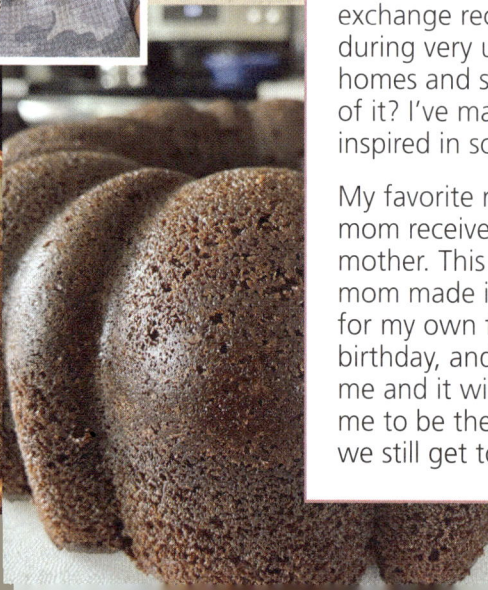

INGREDIENTS

2 cups flour

2 cups sugar

¾ cup cocoa powder

1 teaspoon salt

1 teaspoon baking powder

2 teaspoons baking soda

1 teaspoon vanilla

1 cup milk

1 cup vegetable oil

2 eggs

PLUS 1 cup of brewed coffee

LINDA & TRACY'S CHOCOLATE CAKE

Beat the above ingredients for 1 to 2 minutes (except for the coffee).

SLOWLY mix in 1 cup (brewed) coffee.

Mix for 1-2 minutes on high (batter is very watery, it is supposed to be that way!)

Oil or spray bundt pan very well (I use Pam with Flour). Pour batter in and bake for 35 to 45 minutes (depending on your oven) on 350°F.

Let cake cool for at least 2 hours and then turn over onto flat cake container. Let cool COMPLETELY and sprinkle with confectioner's sugar.

Enjoy!

From the Quarantine Kitchen of
Rosa Etergineoso

INGREDIENTS

3 cups of flour

1 ½ cup of sugar

1 teaspoon of baking powder

1 ½ teaspoons of vanilla

½ teaspoon of salt

1 ½ cup of whole almonds

4 eggs

⅔ cup of unsalted butter, softened at room temperature

¼ teaspoon of almond extract

ALMOND BISCOTTI

Position oven racks in the middle and top of the oven and preheat to 350°F. Line 2 large baking sheets with parchment paper and set aside.

On a separate baking sheet, add the almonds and make sure to spread them in one single layer. Toast them in the oven for about 10 minutes, or until they have toasted up a bit and they are a lovely golden brown color. Allow them to cool a bit and chop them roughly.

In a large bowl, mix together the flour, salt, and baking powder, set aside.

In the bowl of an electric mixer fitted with a paddle attachment, cream together the sugar and butter. Then, add the eggs, almond extract; make sure it's a nice creamy mixture once everything is incorporated.

Add the dry ingredients and mix until it's well incorporated. Add the whole toasted almonds and mix them in well.

Dump the dough onto a heavily floured board and divide into 3 equal portions. Roll each piece into a log that's about 10 inches long and 2 inches wide. Make sure to dust with flour along the way to keep dough from sticking. Set the logs about 4 inches apart onto the prepared baking sheet, press gently to flatten each log just a little with the tips of your fingers. Bake until the logs are golden and firm near the center, about 35 to 40 minutes or until they are lightly golden, but still soft, make sure you are rotating the baking sheets half way through to ensure even baking.

Let the logs cool enough to handle, about 10 minutes. Transfer logs to a cutting board, using a serrated knife, slice them on a sharp diagonal into about 3/4 inch thick slices. Arrange the slices on the baking sheets, laying cut side down. Return to oven and bake for 7 minutes. Turn the cookies over and rotate the baking sheets and bake for another 7 minutes, or until golden and lightly browned.

Let cool on the baking sheets for about 5 minutes before transferring to a wire rack to cool completely. (The cookies will not harden until totally cooled). Enjoy!

HOMEMADE LIMONCELLO

My family has always loved limoncello as an after dinner drink. With my dad's help and some trial and error versions, we came up with a pretty good mixture. Then, we traveled to Italy as a family in 2019. Our grandfather's family members live in Sorrento, Italy, which is one of the main towns in Italy known for their lemons. Lemons are a main ingredient in Sorrento. Fun Fact: 60% of the lemons produced in Italy are used to make limoncello! While in Sorrento, we learned many facts and tips regarding the production of limoncello. We tried different versions and decided that the homemade version made by cousins and friends was always the best! Family members convinced us that zesting the lemons instead of peeling them, was the best way to go. We also learned a few other good tips including buying organic, large lemons, letting the lemon zest sit in the alcohol for a longer time and then allowing the final mixture to rest for several weeks before drinking it so that it truly coagulates and becomes creamy in texture. It was fun to dig into the roots of limoncello, especially knowing our family members live in this very town. Not only do we enjoy drinking it but we also love that it is truly a part of our family heritage and stems from the town of our very own grandfather and ancestors.

Coming from an Italian family, food and drinks were a huge part of life. Everything always seemed to revolve around food. It was always a family event to cook for an occasion, which brought us together. I personally love baking and cooking. My grandfather owned a bakery on Staten Island for many years back in the day. It was called "Pino's." I guess I took on the love of baking from him, who actually learned from his uncle in Sorrento, Italy, where our family still owns a bakery to this day. Baking is therapeutic for me. When I found the Quarantine Kitchen page through a friend, I was so excited. It was truly a distraction from the craziness of the pandemic. I loved seeing all the different foods and recipes that everyone posted. It inspired me to bust out some old recipes and try new recipes, which I love doing. It was amazing to be able to share recipes with so many people. Everyone was always quick to share recipes and I thoroughly enjoyed watching videos of some making their dishes and desserts. Quarantine Kitchen also brought a lot of us together that had the love of cooking and baking in common. I also enjoyed being able to converse with so many people I didn't know about, something I love doing. It brought a lot of joy to me to be part of the group. It also brought some enjoyment to my family who reaped the benefits of all the cooking and baking! Thank you Quarantine Kitchen!

INGREDIENTS

(Fills about 3 ½ bottles)

1 liter bottle of vodka or everclear

2 lemons (organic, if possible)

4 cups sugar

4 cups water

Also needed
Glass or ceramic container that you can close (Plastic containers allow too much air in. I use a dutch oven pot.)

Cheesecloth or coffee filters

Strainer

Zester

Glass brewing bottles/storage bottles

HOMEMADE LIMONCELLO

Step 1
Zest the lemons and put zest in container of your choice. Try to avoid getting the white of the lemons in the zest. (Some peel the lemons. I have found that zesting brings more flavor and color). Once all the lemons are zested, pour the alcohol in the container, stir and cover. Leave for about 30 to 40 days at room temperature. (Leaving for this length of time really gets all the flavor from the zest and allows the flavor and color to mix with the alcohol well. You can stir it up once in a while but do not have to).

Step 2
After sitting for the 30-40 days, make the sugar water by dissolving sugar in water, overheat, but do not boil. Let the sugar water cool to room temperature. In the meantime, strain the lemon zest from the alcohol using a strainer and either a cheesecloth or coffee filter, into a large bowl or pot. If using coffee filters, you may need a few to sift all of the zest and residue out. Strain the liquid a few times to make sure there are no remnants of the zest. Once the sugar water is cooled, add to the alcohol and mix for a couple of minutes. Pour into the glass storage bottles and seal tight. Let it sit in the refrigerator or freezer for 2 to 3 weeks and then enjoy!

Limoncello will last to up to a year if stored in freezer. The longer it sits, the creamier it becomes and better tasting. I usually make 2 times this recipe and it lasts 8 to 12 months, and the bottles that sit for longer are even better than the first few!

From the Quarantine Kitchen of
Angela Catania

A frequent treat when I was growing up was sour cream cinnamon coffee cake.

My mom used to call it "Jewish coffee cake." I guess because it had sour cream? However, I have renamed it.

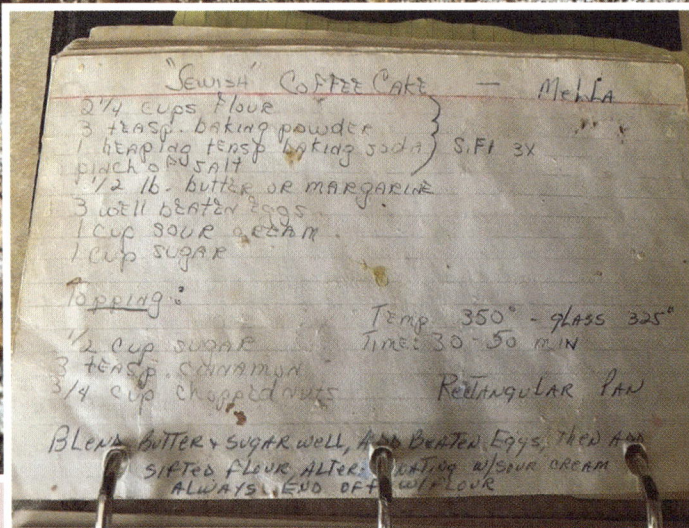

"Jewish" Coffee Cake — Mella

2¼ cups flour
3 teasp. baking powder
1 heaping teasp. baking soda ⎫ S.Fl. 3X
pinch of salt
½ lb. butter or margarine
3 well beaten eggs
1 cup sour cream
1 cup sugar

Topping: Temp. 350° - glass 325°
½ cup sugar   Time: 30 - 50 min
3 teasp. cinnamon
¾ cup chopped nuts   Rectangular pan

Blend butter & sugar well, add beaten eggs, then add
sifted flour alter. beating w/sour cream
always end off w/flour